The quest for mach one

0670874604

The Quest for Mach One

*A First-Person Account of
Breaking the Sound Barrier*

The Quest for Mach One

A First-Person Account of Breaking the Sound Barrier

Chuck Yeager, Bob Cardenas, Bob Hoover,

Jack Russell, and James Young

From oral history interviews
conducted by Dana Marcotte Kilanowski

With commentary by Mac McKendry

Introduction by Walter Boyne

Afterword by Jeffrey Ethell

PENGUIN STUDIO

Published by the Penguin Group

Penguin Putnam Inc., 375 Hudson Street, New York, New York 10014, U.S.A.

Penguin Books Ltd, 27 Wrights Lane, London W8 5TZ, England

Penguin Books Australia Ltd, Ringwood, Victoria, Australia

Penguin Books Canada Ltd, 10 Alcorn Avenue, Toronto, Ontario, Canada M4V 3B2

Penguin Books (N.Z.) Ltd, 182-190 Wairau Road, Auckland 10, New Zealand

Penguin Books Ltd, Registered Offices:
Harmondsworth, Middlesex, England

First published in 1997 by Penguin Studio,
a member of Penguin Putnam Inc.

10 9 8 7 6 5 4 3 2 1

Copyright © Atwood Keeney & Company, Inc.,
Dana Kilanowski, and Flight Test Historical Foundation, 1997
All rights reserved

CIP data available

ISBN 0-670-87460-4

Printed in the United States of America

This book was conceived, researched, and developed for publication by L. Douglas Keeney,
Dana M. Kilanowski, and William S. Butler. They wish to thank the following people and organizations for their assistance and contributions to this project:

The Department of Defense Legacy Resource Management Program; the Men of Mach One—
Brigadier General Charles E. "Chuck" Yeager, USAF (Ret.), Brigadier General Robert L. Cardenas,
USAF (Ret.), Robert A. "Bob" Hoover, Jack Russell, Richard H. Frost, and Eugene S. "Mac"
McKendry; from The Air Force Flight Test Center, Edwards Air Force Base—Colonel James H.
Doolittle III, Vice Commander, and Richard N. Norwood, Historic Preservation Officer; from the
Air Force Flight Test Center History Office—Dr. James O. Young, Chief Historian; Cheryl Gumm,
Deputy Historian; Fred Johnsen, Historian; Dr. Raymond Puffer, Historian; and Joyce Baker, Histor-
ical Assistant/Archivist; from the Air Force Flight Test Center Museum—Doug Nelson and Ilah Nel-
son; from the Flight Test Historical Foundation—J. J. Gianquinto, Esq.; and Robert D. Dennis; and
Mary Strobel; Lt. Col. Samuel J. Kilanowski USAF (Ret.); Joyce A. Chambers; Dr. Barney Oldfield;
and Jeffrey Ethell; The Society of Experimental Test Pilots; and the United States Air Force Test Pilots School; from Penguin Studio—Michael Fragnito, Publisher; and Marie Timell, Senior Editor.

The photographs in this volume and the pages on
which they appear are from the following sources:

Air Force Flight Test Center: v, vi, viii, ix (t), ix (b), x,
xi, xii–xiii, xiv, xv, xvii, xviii, 2, 4, 6-7, 12(b), 13, 14,
15(t&b), 16(b), 20-21, 22, 24, 26-27, 28, 31(t&b), 33,
34, 36-37, 38, 40, 42(b), 44, 45, 46, 47, 49, 50, 51(t&b),
52-53, 54-55, 60(b), 71(t), 80, 83, 84, 85, 86-87(l&r),
88, 89, 90-91, 92, 93, 94-95, 96(t&b), 97(photo by
Jackie Ridley), 98, 100, 102-3, 104, 105, 106, 107, 108,
109, 110, 112, 113, 114(t&b), 116(t&b), 117, 118, 122,
125, 126, 128, 129, 132(t&b), 133, 134, 137, 138

Jack Russell: 3, 10, 12(t), 16(t), 17, 18, 25(t&b), 30, 43,
63

Robert Cardenas: 42(t), 130, 131

Mac McKendry: 56, 58, 59, 60(t), 61, 62, 64, 65, 66, 67,
68(t), 69, 70(t&b), 71(b), 72-73(l&r), 74-75, 76(t&b),
77, 78, 79

Barney Oldfield: 68(b)

Set in Garamond Book
Designed by Jaye Zimet
Page layouts by Kathryn Parise

Contents

Introduction

The History of Flight Testing, by Walter Boyne   vii

Chapter One

The Dawn of Jet-Powered Flight: World War II   1

Chapter Two

Bell Aircraft and the Creation of a Transonic Airplane   11

Chapter Three

The XS-1 Project Moves to Muroc Army Air Field   23

Chapter Four

The Air Force Takes Over the XS-1 Program   29

Chapter Five

The X-1 Team Assembles at Muroc   41

Chapter Six

The Happy Bottom Riding Club   57

Chapter Seven

Powered Flight Testing   81

Chapter Eight

The Day Mach One Is Broken   99

Chapter Nine

The Milestone Realized   111

Afterword

The Men of Mach One, by Jeffrey Ethell   119

Glossary   141

BACKGROUND: An aerial view of Muroc Army Air Field in October 1946. The vast stretches of Rogers Dry Lake, seen to the right just off the end of the runway, gave many a worried test pilot plenty of room to bring in a crippled airplane. Today the base is called Edwards Air Force Base, and it still provides an advantageous spot for flight testing and for landing the Space Shuttles.

The History of Flight Testing

BY WALTER BOYNE

On October 14, 1997, the world will celebrate the fiftieth anniversary of an event that signaled the birth of a new age in aviation, the epic flight of Capt. Charles E. Yeager. In the popular words of 1947, the "twenty-four-year-old World War II ace broke the sound-barrier" in the Bell XS-1 rocket plane *Glamorous Glennis*, named for his wife.

The event was a closely held secret at the time, but word inevitably leaked out that an aircraft had gone beyond Mach 1.0, the speed of sound. The general public applauded the flight, accepting it as just one of a number of wonderful things occurring at a time when nearly every week a new aircraft was flown, a new atomic bomb was tested, or, even more important in the eyes of a consumer-happy country, a new automobile appeared on the market. In the American way, the charismatic Yeager would be vastly better known fifty years later, as he delighted crowds at air shows with his flying.

The flight would probably have had even less impact if it had not dispelled the long-standing myth of an impenetrable barrier in the sky that prevented aircraft from flying beyond the speed of sound. The fact that bullets had been traveling at supersonic speeds for years had never bothered theoreticians whose calculations regularly proved that attempting to penetrate the sound barrier would inevitably cause an aircraft to break up.

The public's relaxed attitude was understandable. World War II had just ended, the United States was the premier aviation power in the world, and it must have seemed only right that a pilot in the brand new United States Air Force (it was less than a month old at the time of the flight) should break the sound barrier. Even within the Air Force, the honor of being the first pilot to fly in excess of Mach 1.0 speed was not overblown. Yeager received the MacKay Trophy (first awarded to Gen. Henry H. "Hap" Arnold) and the Collier Trophy, but, even if his future assignments were considered good ones, his promotions had not accelerated by any

Captain Chuck Yeager, the first man to fly faster than the speed of sound.

Aviation pioneer General Henry H. "Hap" Arnold, chief of the Army Air Corps during World War II, believed that in order for the United States to remain the world leader in air power, it had to maintain a preeminence in flight test research.

means. In general, Yeager was regarded by his peers as a highly competent test pilot who had been given the tools to do a job. He had done the job and *lived,* and that perhaps was considered a more important factor at the time, for it was an age when the lives of test pilots were the currency of progress, and fatalities occurred at a rate that would be considered absolutely unacceptable today.

There was nothing cavalier nor cold-blooded about the approach of manufacturers and governments to the hazards of test flying. Danger was always implicit in flight, and it was considered routine that advancing the progress of flight with new aircraft would always have the possibly fatal element of danger. This attitude was mirrored by the pilots. Everyone knew that test flying was hazardous, and most pilots declined the opportunity to take part. Still, there was never any shortage of test pilots, for there was always a certain breed of man to whom the idea of advancing aviation's progress was made more, rather than less, attractive by the danger. It speaks well for humanity that men (and, later as society caught up, women as well) like these were found in all countries at all times.

In the beginning, of course, all pilots were test pilots, from Otto Lilienthal to the Wright Brothers and beyond. Over time, some inventors and manufacturers, too old or too wise to attempt to fly themselves, hired pilots to fly for them. By World War I there was a recognized need for specialized, if not professional, test

Henry H. "Hap" Arnold.

Larry Bell, Hap Arnold, and Orville Wright. Larry Bell, aviation pioneer and president of Bell Aircraft, was a giant in the aviation industry. Bell Aircraft had manufactured America's first jet, the Bell XP-59 A, which was first flown at Muroc on October 1, 1942. Bell was well respected by his employees and other members of the aviation industry for his personal oversight and involvement in his company's projects. This fact led to Bell's success in the XS-1 project.

Col. Albert G. Boyd with the P-80R, the specially modified Shooting Star in which he flew to 628.8 mph, the first absolute world speed record, set at Muroc on June 19, 1947. Col. Albert Boyd is generally regarded as "the father of USAF Flight Test." As commander of the Flight Test Division at Wright Field, he personally selected Chuck Yeager and other members of the Mach One team for the XS-1 project.

pilots—men who were able to fly a wide variety of new aircraft and assess their strengths and weaknesses. It was a costly process: The opinions of the test pilots were supreme, and they could (and often did) condemn an aircraft not to their liking after a single flight, even when more testing and a moderate amount of development may well have led to a superb design.

By the mid-1930s, flight testing had become a venue of professional pilots, and they had begun to come into their own. There were two main avenues of work. One group worked for the manufacturers, either directly for the company or on a freelance basis. Edward "Eddie" Allen, the acknowledged expert on large aircraft at the time, was under contract to Boeing but was allowed to test aircraft of the other manufacturers as well. Vance Breese was a freelancer, a specialist in first flights. Milo Burcham and Tony LeVier starred for Lockheed, while H. Lloyd Child made headlines for Curtiss.

The other group worked for the armed services or the National Advisory Committee for Aeronautics (NACA). Of course, the military produced great test pilots themselves, including the United States Army Air Force's (USAAF) Stanley Umstead and Albert Boyd, and the Navy's Jack Gorton and Ward Harrigan. NACA test pilot Bill McAvoy became famous for the wide variety of aircraft he tested, which included everything from the four-engine Hall flying boat to fighters to the Lockheed XC-35.

Test pilots in Europe were receiving similar recognition. In Germany, Erich Warsitz was to fly the world's first successful rocket and jet aircraft, the Heinkel He-176 and He-178, respectively. Fritz Wendel became Messerschmitt's chief pilot after setting a world's speed record in the Messerschmitt Me-209R. Great Britain, with its multiplicity of relatively small manufacturers, produced a distinguished list of test pilots, including Westland's Harold Penrose; Vicker's Joseph "Mutt" Summers; De Havilland's Geoffrey de Havilland, Jr.; and Gloster's Philip E. G. Sayer. Even the less powerful nations managed to create their own breed of test pilots.

Test centers also increased in importance. Dayton had long been a test center, first with McCook Field, then Wright Field, and ultimately Wright-Patterson Air Force Base. Ultimately, however, the need for secrecy and space led to the move to Muroc (which later became Edwards Air Force Base), in what was then a remote area of California in the Mojave Desert. The Navy followed a similar path, operating first at Anacostia in Washington, D.C., and the Naval Proving Ground at Dahlgren, Virginia, before moving to Cedar Point, Maryland, to establish the Patuxent River Naval Air Test Center. NACA had facilities at Langley, Virginia, for years, but soon began to look to Muroc as well.

One could say that Chuck Yeager and his work in many ways symbolized a transition point in the history of test pilots as much as his historic flight did in the realm of aerodynamics. He epitomized the old school of test pilots, those who depended upon intuitive flying skills to test hot new aircraft and survive. Yet, despite his lack of a college education, he was both intelligent and wise enough to learn to use all the tools and techniques of scientific testing just becoming available in the U.S. Air Force flight test programs. The competence Yeager developed in research then qualified him to become commandant of the USAF Aerospace Research Pilot School (ARPS) in 1962, perhaps the highest honor to which a test pilot can aspire.

The October 14, 1947, manned flight came at a unique point in history. The previous years had witnessed a steady buildup of aeronautic knowledge, growth that had been vastly accelerated by the war. With few exceptions, when World War II began, first-line aircraft of all nations followed a fairly typical formula. They were generally all metal monoplanes of moderate dimensions and weight, with one to four reciprocating engines, and featured enclosed cockpits, retractable landing gear, simple communications gear, and machine guns or cannons for armament. The exigencies of war ensured that millions of dollars, pounds, marks, francs, lira, and yen were spent to speed development. During the six years of the war, a design revolution took place. Swept-wing aircraft with turbojet engines were developed, along with a variety of relatively primitive air-to-air missiles and a surprisingly sophisticated ballistic missile system. Communication, radar, and electronic counter-measures equipment grew extremely complex. Aircraft, having grown much larger and heavier, demanded an infrastructure of airports, depots, weather stations, and similar ancillary services on a previously undreamed-of scale.

At the peak of this development, the war mercifully ended in a great Allied victory that saw all the major combatant countries of the world—with the single exception of the United States—exhausted. The Axis nations were, of course, in the worst straits, because in the process of losing the war, their countries were subjected to ferocious bombardment. But "victors" like Great Britain, France, and the Soviet Union were in equally critical states.

The thrust toward aviation's future might well have come to a complete halt, but there is an unquenchable thirst for knowledge and adventure that persuaded the victorious Allies to pursue research and development to any extent that was possible. Thus in renascent France there appeared such remarkable aircraft as the Leduc ram jets and Sud Quest 9000 Trident. Great Britain pressed forward with the De Havilland DH-108, in which Geoffrey de Havilland, Jr., seeking the sound barrier, lost his life. The British also developed the Fairey F.D. 1 delta-wing research aircraft and a host of other prototypes that led to operational aircraft. The British had actually begun work on a supersonic aircraft in 1943

Chuck Yeager meets Lt. Gen. Laurence C. "Bill" Craigie, the Air Forces' first military jet pilot and chief of the Engineering Division at Wright Field from 1945 to 1947.

The X-series planes had a noble and long lineage. Moreover, the B-29, the mothership for the X-1, was not the only aircraft to carry them aloft—the B-50 bomber was also used as a mothership. Here one takes off for a test flight. Although the B-29 and B-50 look very much alike, there were hundreds of differences, both large and small, between them. The B-50 had bigger, more powerful engines; in fact, less than 25 percent of the parts of one model were interchangeable with the other. Bob Cardenas, the original mothership pilot of the program, never flew the B-50, despite its use in the X-1 program.

with the Miles M-52, an aircraft with remarkable similarities to the Bell XS-1. Thin wings were midset into a bullet-shaped body and an all-moving slab tail was fitted. The project was abandoned prematurely, and British industry was faced with a void of knowledge about the very transonic flight regime it was entering.

The Soviet Union, despite its grievous wounds, was rapidly integrating German technology with its own flourishing industry, with the emphasis placed more on the development of warplanes than on basic research.

The United States was the only country with the resources to apply to a program to create a supersonic aircraft. That it did so was not a matter of luck, but rather because of the inspiration and leadership provided by General of the Army Henry H. "Hap" Arnold. Arnold was a talker rather than a scientist, but he had the insight to realize that if the USAAF's success in World War II had depended upon technology, then the future success of the new USAF would be even more dependent. To address this need for technology, he created what became known as the Scientific Advisory Board, headed by Dr. Theodor von Kármán. An extremely distinguished group of scientists was invited to join the board. Instructed to place less emphasis on the past and to concentrate on future possibilities, they created a report entitled *Toward New Horizons,* which covered everything from aerodynamics to terminal ballistics. Arnold also fostered a culture of research and development in the nascent USAF by seeing that young, vigorous officers were chosen for high positions, regardless of seniority. Thus it was that the new United States Air Force found itself led by men like Hoyt Vandenberg, Laurence Kuter, and Lauris Norstad, who in turn selected bright up-and-coming officers like Bernard Schreiver for top jobs.

It was the combination of funds and leadership that permitted the USAF to join with NACA to place tremendous emphasis on research and development, so that whole generations of X-planes, from the XS-1 to the X-15 and beyond were conceived at a relatively early date and rapidly placed into service. The USAF and the Navy were also each developing an entire series of modern jet combat aircraft, applying the immediate postwar technology of swept wings and jet engines to new applications, and enhancing them with advanced new ideas, such as Richard Whitcomb's area-ruled fuselage, boundary layer control, fly by-wire flight control systems, and a host of others. The combination of experimental work and practical service testing at what would become Edwards Air Force Base began one of the most exciting periods of aviation history. And so it is clear that Yeager's epochal flight was far more than an important engineering event: It was the key to the future, as it accelerated progress in the demanding realm of supersonic flight at a rate that defied past experience.

At a 1947 summit meeting of sorts on the lake bed at Muroc, X-1 pilot Chuck Yeager talks with flying legend Hap Arnold (*center, in hat*). Arnold was instrumental in creating a research capability within the Air Force and turning Muroc into a base dedicated solely to flight testing.

Chuck Yeager (*left*) **and Jackie Ridley** (*right*) **flank Lt. Col. Fred J. Ascani, Col. Albert Boyd's deputy at the Flight Test Division at Wright Field.**

Consider the rapid pace of events. It took just under forty-four years from the Wright Brothers' first successful, controlled, powered flight on December 17, 1903, to Yeager's October 14, 1947, Mach 1.05 success. A little over six years later, on November 20, 1953, the irrepressible Scott Crossfield flew the Navy's Douglas D-558-2 Skyrocket to Mach 2. Less than a month later, Yeager achieved Mach 2.44 in the Bell X-1A. Capt. Frank Everest briefly became the "fastest man alive" with a Mach 2.87 flight on July 23, 1956. Sadly enough, Capt. Milburn Apt next carried the Bell X-2 to Mach 3.196 on September 27, 1956, but was killed when he lost control of the aircraft. Test flying was getting faster but no less dangerous.

The quick rise in speeds went on with the X-15, which Capt. Robert White took to Mach 6 on November 9, 1961, a little over fourteen years after Yeager's flight. The X-15's ultimate speed of Mach 6.7 was achieved on August 21, 1967, by Capt. William "Pete" Knight, and represented thirteen years of incredible progress in aerodynamics, metallurgy, engines, fuels, telemetry, test equipment, and a hundred scientific disciplines. If either Bell or Yeager had failed, such progress might have been delayed by a decade or more.

The test pilots and their famous X-planes were a prelude to the manned space program, and indeed, several test pilots qualified as astronauts. Robert White became the first to do this by reaching an altitude of 314,750 feet in the X-15 on July 17, 1962. Six other pilots would achieve that distinction in the X-15.

As the age of the computer presses in on us ever more tightly, it is important to remember how important the human interface was during the pioneering efforts. All of the pilots of the early XS-1 program—from Jack Woolams to Chalmers "Slick" Goodlin to Yeager—were not only expert aviators, they were a part of a man-machine interface that saved the program on numerous occasions. They set a precedent for the many test pilots and the many test planes that would follow. Fortunately, the engineers of the time were receptive to their input and factored their observations into the design process.

That same human factors of this golden era at Muroc, when Yeager was putting the *Glamorous Glennis* into the history books, saw to it that the appropriate technological spin-offs accrued to combat aircraft. The adjustable horizontal stabilizer on the XS-1 (later the X-1) proved to be of decisive combat advantage when applied to the North American F-86. Ejection seat development was given a tremendous boost by Scott Crossfield's suggestion during the design of the X-15. Over time, other test pilots would prove the validity of other theories, as when Convair test pilot Richard Johnson took the "coke-bottle-fuselage" YF-102A supersonic on its first flight, proving Richard Whitcomb's area rule theory that certain shapes of the fuselage create less drag and therefore more speed.

It would be tempting, from the vantage point of fifty years, to look back on the era of Chuck Yeager and the X-1 and make some philosophical commentary to the effect that "they don't make them like that anymore." But the truth is far different. The true heritage of Yeager and the X-1 lies less in the development of the magnificent hardware that followed the October 14 flight than the formulation of the rich tradition of rigorous science, demanding flying, and utter integrity that has subsequently characterized the Air Force Flight Test Center at Edwards, and indeed,

American test flying in general. The earnest spirit of those early postwar years has permeated the culture of American aviation, as remarkable aircraft like the Lockheed SR-71 and F-117 and the Northrop B-2 attest. That culture is now enhanced—some would say enveloped—by another necessary culture, that of the high-speed computer, with all its ramifications for design and test.

But after all the designing and engineering is done, and regardless of the number of computers on board, there still remains that moment when the test pilot is sitting at the end of the runway, preparing to make the first flight. It is then that the heritage of Chuck Yeager and his colleagues, built so carefully and at such cost in life and treasure for fifty years, asserts itself. And it is at that moment when it becomes obvious that the years of effort, sacrifice, and success that began on October 14, 1947, have been eminently worthwhile.

Boyd (*second from left*) with Yeager (*sixth from left*) during one of the rare formal dress functions at Muroc.

Chapter One

The Dawn of Jet-Powered Flight: World War II

James Young The remarkably rapid evolution of aircraft design during the first four decades of the twentieth century came to an apparent impasse by the late 1930s. While aircraft design engineers had begun to dream of aircraft capable of speeds in excess of 500 miles per hour, some truly daunting challenges faced them. At 500 mph, they would be probing the lower limits of the transonic region, the little-understood area between Mach 0.8 and Mach 1.2, where an aircraft would encounter mixed subsonic and supersonic airflow. As the aircraft approached the speed of sound, Mach 1.0, a virtual "wall" of air would build up in front of it. One prominent aerodynamicist, speaking for many of his colleagues, likened the wall to a "barrier against future progress."

Theoretical calculations seemed to indicate that as an aircraft approached Mach 1.0, drag would reach infinity. Just how much power, scientists wondered, would be required to contend with "infinite drag"? There were other, equally perplexing problems surrounding the phenomenon aerodynamicists called "compressibility." At transonic speeds, an aircraft would encounter variable subsonic and supersonic airflow conditions. Because airflow accelerates as it passes over an airfoil, an airplane may be flying at only seven tenths of the speed of sound, but the flow over its wings may well be moving at supersonic speeds. In this turbulent region of mixed-flow conditions, aerodynamicists knew that shock waves would form on the aircraft and, moving back and forth, violently disrupt the airflow and dramatically alter the airplane's controllability. Many experts believed the turbulent flow could result in aircraft oscillations severe enough to cause structural damage.

The magnitude of the problem was brought home in terrifying fashion one morning in November 1941, when veteran Lockheed test pilot Ralph Virden pushed over into a steep dive in a P-38 "Lightning." As he accelerated, he lost elevator effectivencss, and the P-38's dive angle grew increasingly steep. As the craft picked up speed, ultimately to about 535 mph, the violently disturbed airflow com-

Chuck Yeager was a fighter pilot and an "Ace" in World War II. Bob Cordenas said "Chuck has eyesight like an eagle; he could spot the enemy several seconds before they could see him. His eyesight gave him a remarkable edge in combat."

As with his other planes before this, Chuck Yeager named his P-51 fighter *Glamorous Glen,* after his wife, Glennis. He later named the XS-1 the *Glamorous Glennis*, for good luck, shortly before his first supersonic flight.

ing off the wings overstressed the tail and literally tore it off. Caught in the grip of compressibility, a skillful test pilot had been reduced to the role of helpless passenger on a journey toward destruction.

Throughout World War II, pilots of high-performance fighters continued to encounter this problem. During high-speed dives, they would suddenly discover that their control columns had frozen or reversed direction altogether. Even if they were ultimately able to effect abrupt dive recoveries, the excessive aerodynamic loads imposed on the tails of their aircraft all too frequently resulted in catastrophic failures.

All of these very serious problems surfaced while propeller-driven fighters still ruled supreme. The greater flying speeds that came with the development of turbojet technology during the war years made the search for a real solution to compressibility all the more compelling. By war's end, it was obvious that turbojet engines offered the potential to propel aircraft through the transonic—and, perhaps, even into the supersonic—region. The major question was: Could a piloted aircraft be designed and built to survive compressibility? The answer, unfortunately, was not easily forthcoming.

Chuck Yeager After my return to America from World War II in 1945, I was assigned by the Air Force to be the assistant maintenance officer in the Fighter Test Section of the Flight Test Division at Wright Field, in Dayton, Ohio. As a maintenance officer, it was my job to run functional flight tests on all of the aircraft in the Fighter Test Section when they came out of maintenance work. There I saw, got to sit in, then fly my first jet aircraft, the Bell P-59.

My first impression of the jet was how smooth the engines were compared to the quick-acceleration piston engines of the P-51s. The controls on a jet are almost the same as those on a P-51 or on a conventional engine-powered fighter. You simply push forward on the throttle and the airplane goes. But a jet aircraft is a little bit slower on acceleration, and a little bit touchier on landing, since the transition time from approach speed to touchdown speed is longer in a jet. All in all, though, that P-59 was really a lot of fun to fly.

Larry Bell in the XP-59-A (photo autographed to Jack Russell).

Fighter pilot Chuck Yeager during World War II with his P-51 Mustang *Glamorous Glen*.

That was not my first experience with jets, however. This came in 1944 when I was a pilot with the 357th Fighter Group, a P-51 Mustang outfit flying out of England against the Germans. It was the summer of 1944 and I was escorting a flight of bombers near Bremen, Germany. There were four of us fighters, and we were looking for targets of opportunity at an altitude of 15,000 feet. Suddenly, 12 to 15 miles in front of me, I spotted three aircraft. They were lower than I was, down around 8,000 feet. I really did not know what they were. They were coming around the one o'clock position going 180 degrees toward me. I put the nose of the P-51 down and went to full power on the engine. I was up to 460 mph indicated. I pulled in, trying to get a deflection shot on the lead aircraft. I got within 1,000 yards of him, but all of a sudden he pulled away from me like I was standing still. We had been briefed on jet aircraft—what they looked like and some of their performance characteristics—but when I saw one in person, how fast it was came as a complete surprise. Speed or no speed, I was anxious to tangle with those aircraft, so I hung around the general area and finally spotted one trying to land on an airfield. I maneuvered into a split S and pulled in behind him. He had his gear down and was about two miles on final approach to the runway when I opened fire at about 200 yards and closed in very fast. He blew up as he approached the end of the runway.

It did not take a genius to see that jet propulsion was soon going to take over the aviation business. It did not escape the notice of American aircraft manufacturers, either, and right after the war, developments in jet technology accelerated. The Air Force had been convinced of the superiority of jet propulsion since facing the German jets in the late stages of the war, and had been pushing for an American design for some time. Being in the Air Corps Fighter Test Section, in August 1945, I was sent to Edwards Air Force Base—then called Muroc Air Base, at Rogers Dry Lake in California—to conduct the first engine service test of a jet called the P-80. While there, flying the P-80s, I got to know them quite well.

We advanced from P-80s to P-84s. The P-84 was the first airplane I had flown that had the capability of flying up to its structural speed limit, around .82 Mach, on a straight and level flight. It also was the aircraft in which I first experienced some of the flying characteristics of the transonic region. The P-84 would fly straight and level at .82 Mach. But if I tried to go faster, the airplane would buffet—that is, shake to the point of loss of control—and pitch up. This could occur in all of our straight-wing jet aircraft of that era. The buffeting was a characteristic of an effect called compressibility, and compressibility was the big obstacle to breaking the sound barrier.

My first experience with compressibility was in 1944, in combat, flying the P-51 against the German Me-109 and Focke-Wulf 190 fighter planes. During combat in those days, if you got on the tail of a 190 or 109 (if the pilot did not bail out), he would head for the deck going as fast as he could. Chasing them would accelerate the P-51 up to .81 Mach by flying straight down from high altitude. At that speed I encountered the aerodynamic effect of compressibility. A shock wave would form on the wings and would cause buffeting and a significant decrease in the pilot's ability to control the aircraft.

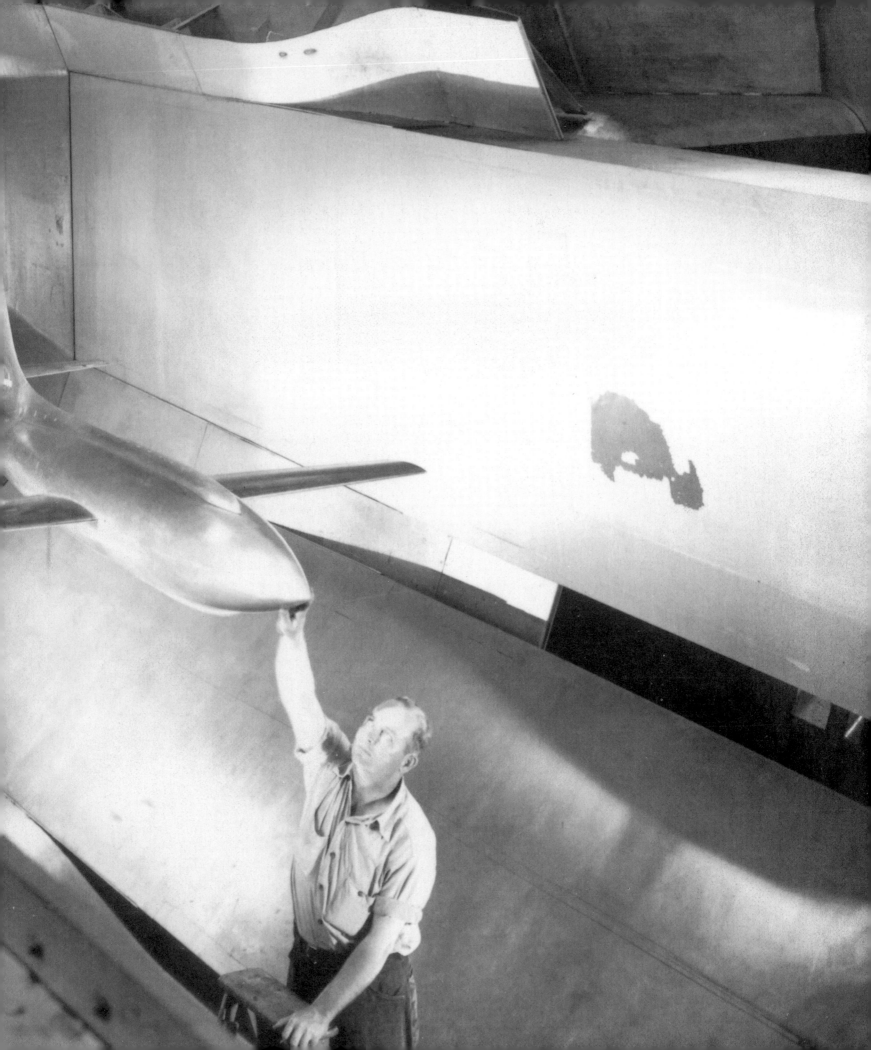

At that time we didn't know a lot about the causes of compressibility but later we learned fast. Smarter people than Air Force combat pilots at Bell Aircraft Corporation and the National Advisory Committee for Aeronautics (NACA) were aware of the problems associated with approaching the speed of sound and had already conceived of the idea to build an aircraft that could not just survive but fly comfortably in the region of the speed of sound.

James Young To break the sound barrier, aircraft designers needed complete knowledge of transonic aerodynamics—knowledge based on concrete evidence, not theoretical calculations. Throughout the war years, however, wind tunnels, traditionally used to measure airflow conditions around airplane models, remained practically useless for transonic research. At Mach levels below 0.7 and above 1.3, smooth airflow through tunnels could be maintained, and thus aerodynamicists could acquire accurate measurements. But, between 0.8 and 1.2 Mach, the tunnels "choked," as shock waves formed on test models and then reflected off tunnel walls, thereby inhibiting accurate measurement of flow characteristics around the model. The best solution to this problem, the slotted-throat transonic tunnel, would not arrive on the scene until the late 1940s.

In the meantime, other methods of data acquisition—rocket-propelled models, free-falling instrumented missile shapes released at high altitudes, and wingflow tests of airfoil shapes mounted on the upper surface of aircraft wings—were employed as stopgap alternatives. Although some useful data was acquired by these means, it was really of limited value in terms of the magnitude of the problems to be overcome. These circumstances enhanced the appeal of a far more radical approach: to build and flight test a fully instrumented experimental aircraft. Such an approach would represent a radical departure from standard practice; in essence, a reversal of the time-honored process wherein researchers accumulated and analyzed data *before* the designers built their aircraft. There were legions of experts who scoffed at this approach, but there were others who labored long and hard to promote its merits. Three men in particular would play pivotal roles in the genesis of the experimental research airplane programs of the mid- to late '40s: John Stack, director of the Compressibility Research Division at the National Advisory Committee for Aeronautics' (NACA) Langley Laboratory; Maj. Ezra Kotcher, chief of aeronautical research for the U.S. Army Air Forces at Wright Field; and Capt. Walter S. Diehl, who, for years, served as the Navy Bureau of Aeronautics de facto representative to NACA. Each of these men were confident that the sonic "wall" could be breached, and each strove to convince their respective organizations that research airplanes offered the best means to convince the aeronautical community that, in Captain Diehl's words, the "sound barrier" was "just a steep hill."

Their dogged persistence finally began to yield results when, on March 15, 1944, each of the military services engaged in separate meetings with NACA personnel at Langley. Although all three organizations had finally agreed on the need for a transonic research aircraft, there was little agreement among them concerning the basic design features of such a craft or even the specific goals for a flight test program. NACA, which could not fund such a program, needed support from

PREVIOUS SPREAD: **The engineers at the National Advisory Committee for Aeronautics (NACA) at Langley Field, near Washington, utilize a sixteen-foot high-speed tunnel to test the aerodynamics of the XS-1 shape.**

the military services. As negotiations proceeded, however, prospects for a single, concerted effort evaporated because of a fundamental disagreement over the best means to approach a transonic research program. Following NACA's lead, and John Stack's views, the Navy favored a cautious approach utilizing jet propulsion in a very gradual, step-by-step program directed toward the acquisition of transonic data. The Army, however, at Ezra Kotcher's prompting, remained convinced that rocket propulsion offered far superior high-speed performance—800 mph performance—that could enable an airplane to quickly dispel the sound-barrier myth.

Stack and NACA were staunchly opposed to the rocket-propulsion proposal, insisting that the immaturity of the technology made such an approach far too dangerous. Stack informed Kotcher that the majority of NACA Langley test pilots would be unwilling to fly in a rocket-powered aircraft. Privately, in fact, Melvin Gough, NACA's chief test pilot at Langley, had issued an edict: "No NACA pilot will ever be permitted to fly an airplane powered by a damned firecracker!" Stack also argued that such a craft could not offer enough endurance (only a couple of minutes of powered flight per mission) to yield either the kind or the volume of data that flight researchers required. Besides, data derived from a turbojet configuration would obviously be more directly applicable to aviation's near-term future. Kotcher and the Army, however, remained firm in their commitment to a rocket-powered vehicle and, by December 1944, were looking for a contractor to build it. Since the Army was procuring the airplane, NACA had little choice but to acquiesce and begin preparations for its support of the program.

Chapter Two

Bell Aircraft and the Creation of a Transonic Airplane

James Young The Bell Aircraft Corporation agreed to take on the job of developing the Army's airplane in December 1944. The basic requirements for the aircraft seemed straightforward enough:

- the rocket engine should have at least a two-minute endurance capability;
- the aircraft would have to be able to attain 800 mph at 35,000 feet;
- it would be unencumbered from all of the usual military specifications;
- its structural components should be manufactured especially strong for safety;
- its safety and controllability had to be guaranteed up to a speed of Mach 0.8.

The requirements may have been straightforward, but as the Bell team began to undertake its preliminary design studies, its members quickly discovered what it felt like to be set adrift on an uncharted sea. Two of them, design engineer Benson Hamlin and aerodynamicist Paul Emmons, traveled to various research facilities around the country in search of useful data and expert advice. They found little of either. Hamlin later recalled commenting to Emmons on the train ride back to the Bell facility in Buffalo, New York, that they were basically free to design the aircraft "any way we please, and no one can criticize us."

NACA's most important contributions to the design of the airplane centered on the horizontal stabilizer (the horizontal portion of an airplane's tail section), which the committee insisted should be thinner than the wings. Thus, if the wings encountered serious compressibility effects at a certain speed, the thinner stabilizer with its higher critical Mach number would not lose its effectiveness by simultaneously encountering the same problems. In the event of serious stability and control problems, this would permit the pilot to maintain adequate control of the airplane until he could decelerate to a lower Mach number. In order to guarantee sufficient

Two famous Bell test pilots, Jack Woolams (*left*) and Alvin M. "Tex" Johnston, flew the X-1 before the reins were handed to Slick Goodlin, then to Chuck Yeager. Here Woolams and Johnston are on the XP-59A "Airacomet," America's first jet.

The core of the Bell Aircraft Corporation. President Larry Bell (*left*) and chief test pilot Bob Stanley.

The X-1's rocket engine, the XLR-11, designed by Reaction Motors. The X-1 underwent test launches and glide flights at Pinecastle, Florida, before these engines were finally installed.

longitudinal control in the transonic region, NACA also recommended mounting the elevator (the moveable flight control surface at the rear of a horizontal stabilizer that controls the pitch movement of an aircraft's nose) on an adjustable rather than fixed horizontal stabilizer. At subsonic speeds, the pilot could employ the elevator for adequate control. In the transonic region, however, he could opt to change the stabilizer's angle of incidence. Finally, NACA stipulated that the horizontal stabilizer should be located high on the vertical fin in order to minimize wing-wake impingement on it.

The Army finally settled on a 6,000-pound-thrust rocket engine, which had originally been under development for the Navy by Reaction Motors, Inc. The XLR-11 was a four-cylinder engine (1,500 pounds of thrust per cylinder) that employed liquid oxygen and diluted ethyl alcohol as propellants. Though not throttleable, the pilot would have the option to ignite or shut down each cylinder individually so that he could operate at 25, 50, 75, or 100 percent power.

Unfortunately, the development of a turbine-driven dual-propellant pump originally intended for use on the craft was plagued by so many problems that it had to be sidelined. Replacing it would be a system in which high-pressure nitrogen gas would be used to force-feed the liquid oxygen and alcohol into the engine. With the internal pressure of the nitrogen gas at 350 pounds per square inch, heavy, high-strength steel containers would have to be designed into the aircraft. Not only would the tanks be heavier, but their almost spherical shapes would be far less efficient in terms of volume than the low-pressure cylindrical aluminum tanks that would have been used with a turbine-pumped system. Propellant storage capacity was further reduced because the nitrogen used to pressurize the propellant system would also have to be stored in a group of heavy, high-pressure tanks. A total of twelve of these 4,800 psi nitrogen containers, along with three heavy-duty regulators and two smaller regulators, would be required onboard. The impact of all this on the aircraft's design was critical: The vehicle's landing weight was increased by one ton, while fuel capacity was reduced from 8,160 pounds to 4,680 pounds. Instead of an engine burn time of 4.2 minutes, the duration would be just 2.4 minutes.

While the reduced engine burn time created a number of headaches for the design team, it at least served to resolve a very contentious debate over whether the aircraft should be designed for air launch or ground takeoff. NACA and a number of Bell personnel had argued vehemently in favor of ground takeoffs. NACA favored this approach because it would provide useful data on the widest possible range of conventional flight operations. Those Bell management personnel who agreed with this approach did so because they were looking toward the future development of the craft into a rocket-powered interceptor. Key members of the design team, most notably Robert Stanley and Benson Hamlin, countered these arguments by citing safety considerations and the need to conserve rocket propellants for

The Bell Aircraft Corporation plant was located in Niagara Falls, New York, where it had a test hangar. Here the number two X-1 test fires its XLR-11 rocket engine in the hangar. This engine's 6,000 pounds of thrust were eclipsed later by the XLR-25 engine, with its 15,000 pounds of thrust, which was used in the X-2.

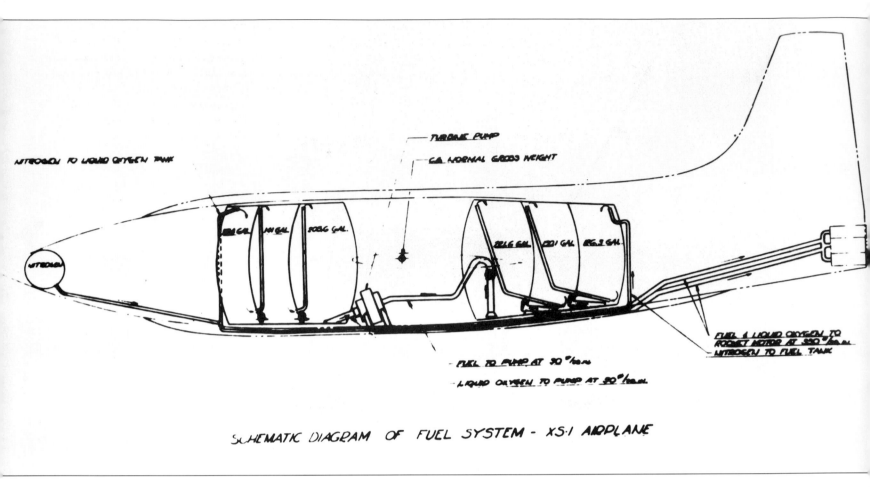

SCHEMATIC DIAGRAM OF FUEL SYSTEM - XS-1 AIRPLANE

A schematic drawing of the liquid oxygen fuel system of the XS-1.

actual high-speed work at altitude as compelling reasons for air launching the craft. Much to NACA's chagrin, the weight increase and reduction in fuel capacity caused by the high-pressure fuel-feed system settled the issue; the research airplane would be air launched at relatively high altitude from the bomb bay of a specially modified B-29 bomber.

While engine and fuel-system problems were being worked out, the designers' attention turned to aerodynamic shape. During their generally disappointing tour of research institutions in the United States, Hamlin and Emmons had made a stop at the U.S. Army Air Forces Ballistics Laboratory at Wright Field, near Dayton, Ohio. They knew that bullets often traveled at supersonic speeds and wondered, specifically, how and why the shape for fifty-caliber bullets (which were known to travel at speeds as high as 2,491 mph) had been determined. They discovered that the specific shape of a bullet's nose had been selected because, in testing, it had produced the smallest dispersion pattern. Here at least was a configuration that had proven to be stable at supersonic speeds. Feeling that they were on to something, and with a paucity of other useful precedents, they decided to pattern the shape of the fuselage after the bullet.

The electrical panel *(top)* and the instrument panel *(bottom)* of the X1-A. The X1-A was the first successor to the X-1 and incorporated subtle refinements that both test pilots and engineers alike embraced. These included a remarkably accessible electrical panel and a more pilot-friendly cockpit layout and instrument cluster.

Jack Woolams (*center, in plaid shirt*) was the first Bell XS-1 test pilot. With him is Crew Chief Jack Russell. After Woolams died in a crash at the Cleveland Air Races, Bell Aircraft named Slick Goodlin as chief test pilot. Woolams was a highly regarded pilot and certainly would have broken the sound barrier had he lived.

Ultimately, after much debate, it was decided that the XS-1 would have to be launched from the air. Boeing manufactured the B-29 bomber that Bell modified to act as the mother ship for the XS-1. Here the XS-1 is shackled to the B-29.

To overcome the problems inherent in building the extremely thin wing needed to reduce drag but still be capable of sustaining 18G loads, the Bell team eventually decided to clad the wings with exceptionally thick aluminum, tapering from one half inch thick at the wing roots to a conventional thickness at the tips. The thick skins would not only add structural integrity and rigidity to the wings, they would also presumably maintain their smooth contours as turbulent flow developed in the transonic flight regime.

Bell test pilot Tex Johnston in the cockpit of the P-59. Alongside is Jack Russell, who went on to become crew chief on the X-1 project.

Wind-tunnel testing of the X-1 at Bell Aircraft. Although many design characteristics could be analyzed in the tunnel, the critical ones could be tested only with real flying. For example, the concept of the X-1's "flying wing," or adjustable horizontal stabilizer, resulted from actual test flight rather than from laboratory theory.

Working in the same fashion as demonstrated by the American aircraft industry throughout the recent war, the Bell team worked fast and effectively as it solved these and a host of other perplexing problems. The official contract for final design and construction of three XS-1 aircraft (for Experimental Sonic–1; the designation was later simplified to X-1) had been issued on March 16, 1945. Less than ten months later, on December 27, the first aircraft, serial number 46-062, was rolled out of the Bell plant in Niagara Falls, New York.

The Army had selected Pinecastle Field, near Orlando, Florida, as the site for the airplane's initial unpowered glide-flight program. There, carrying ballast instead of its rocket engine, which was not yet ready for installation, the number one XS-1 was carried aloft by the modified B-29 (serial number 45-21800) for a captive test on January 21, 1946. Four days later, on January 25, Bell's chief test pilot, Jack Woolams, was seated in the cockpit of the XS-1 as, at 27,000 feet, it was released from the bomb bay of the B-29 for the first time. Woolams reported a clean break from the B-29 and, ultimately attaining a top speed of approximately 275 mph, thoroughly enjoyed himself during the ten-minute glide to the field below. Reporting that the aircraft felt "solid as a rock" and yet "light as a feather during maneuvers," because of the effectiveness and light balance of the controls, he found the sleek experimental aircraft extremely easy to fly.

Woolams completed a total of ten glide flights at Pinecastle between January and early March 1946. Extremely pleased with the results, Bell ferried the craft back to New York for installation of its engine and to replace the 10-percent wing used during the recent tests with the thin 8-percent wing, which would be employed on the craft during the powered flight portion of its test program. Unfortunately, Woolams, who had fully expected to make those flights, was killed in an accident on August 30, 1946.

Jack Russell My experience with the X-1 goes all the way back to the beginning, so I knew all the test pilots who flew it. Jack Woolams was the first chief test pilot, and unfortunately he was killed in the Cleveland Air Races. Jack was a real ace in the cockpit, but there was nothing flamboyant about him. He was down-to-earth, and I am sure that he would have flown the X-1 supersonic for little or nothing; money did not mean that much to Jack. He was just in it for the job. I think it would have been Woolams who broke the sound barrier, if he had lived.

James Young With resumption of the flight test program close at hand, Bell selected twenty-three-year-old Chalmers H. "Slick" Goodlin to replace Woolams as the XS-1 pilot. Bell was contractually obligated to test the craft and prove its flight worthiness out to 0.8 Mach. It was common practice for the contractor's pilots to fly all of the early, more hazardous phases of test programs. There was no reason to believe that, if he and the XS-1 survived, the Bell pilot would not proceed on to fly the rest of the program up to, and including, the assault on Mach 1.0. In fact, at the outset of the program, the U.S. Army Air Forces had considered issuing Bell a contract to complete the accelerated research phase of the test program.

Jack Russell Bob Stanley was the chief pilot in the flight test group at Bell that contained Bud Kelly, Tex Johnston, Slick Goodlin, Jack Woolams, and a few others. But Slick was selected for the job of flying the X-1 after Jack died. Slick was a real neat guy, a natural-born pilot. He could do amazing things with an airplane. Because he'd flown on aircraft carriers, he was used to landing an airplane in a shorter distance than most everybody. Slick was a very good pilot, but got a little Hollywood-ish because he had the use of a P-51 from Bell, and he'd fly back and forth to Los Angeles and sometimes you didn't know whether he was going to make it back for the next flight or not. He was a real happy-go-lucky kid, a flamboyant guy, but he wasn't that good on the details of his flight programs, as test pilots are supposed to be.

In June 1946, the new number one X-1 stands on the tarmac at Wright Field, Dayton, Ohio, headquarters of the Flight Test Division of the Air Materiel Command.

James Young The potential risks of those upcoming flights were tragically highlighted less than a month after Jack Woolams's fatal accident when, on September 27, English test pilot Geoffrey de Havilland, Jr., was killed during an attempt to set a new world speed record in *The Swallow*. The DH-108 experimental jet was flying in the dense lower atmosphere at only 7,500 feet when, as de Havilland attained a speed of 0.875 Mach, the aircraft was subjected to violent longitudinal pitching oscillations and literally disintegrated. The news was sobering, indeed. By that time, in fact, Great Britain had already abandoned its attempts to develop piloted supersonic research airplanes.

While the British experience gave cause for caution, it did not diminish the confidence of those who, across the Atlantic, were preparing the XS-1 for its powered flights. They believed that the longitudinal oscillations that had claimed *The Swallow* could be controlled by the rocket plane's moveable horizontal stabilizer. And, unlike Geoffrey de Havilland, the pilot of the XS-1 would be doing his speed work in the thinner air of high altitudes where the aircraft would not encounter the severe airloads that had destroyed the British jet.

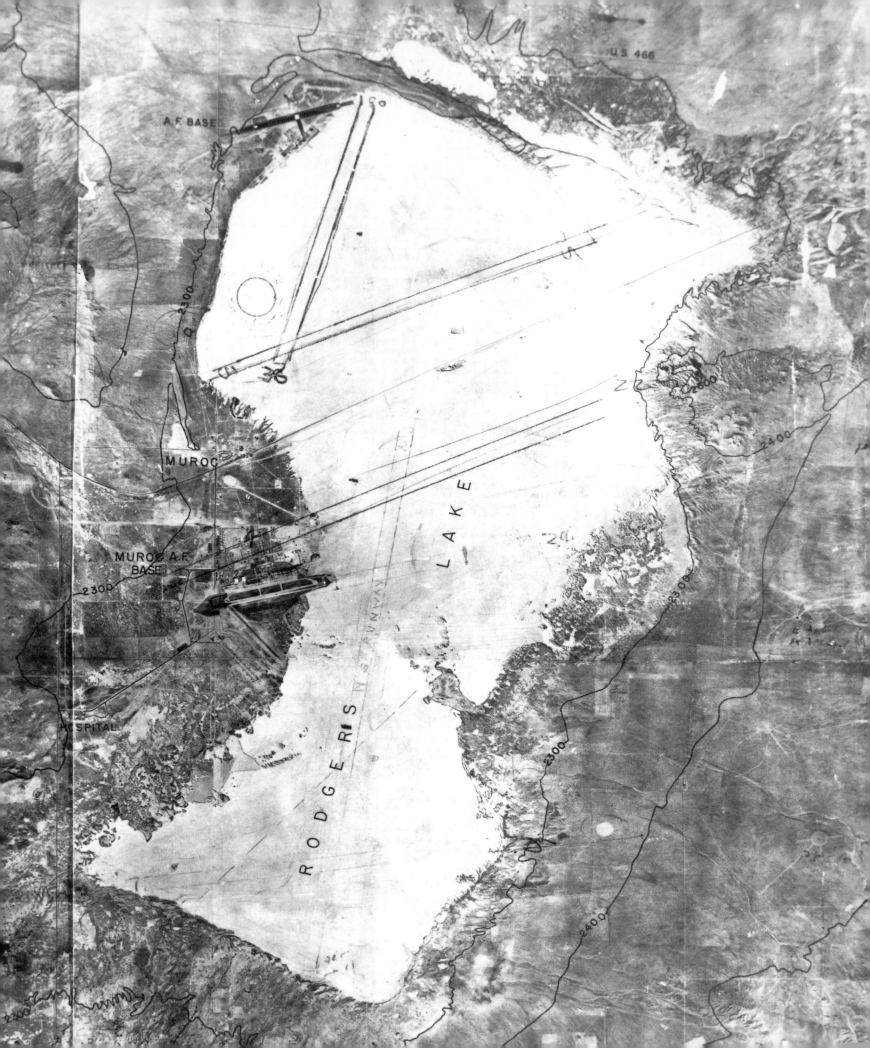

Chapter Three

The XS-1 Project Moves to Muroc Army Air Field

James Young While the Pinecastle glide flights were still under way, the U. S. Army Air Forces decided that the powered flight program should be conducted at an out-of-the-way site on California's high desert. The location selected, Muroc Army Air Field, had proven to be ideal for the purposes of testing high-performance aircraft. Back in 1942, it had been selected as the site for the initial flights of this country's first jet aircraft, the Bell XP-59A "Airacomet," because it offered the advantages of excellent year-round flying weather, complete isolation, and the incalculable margin of safety afforded by the availability of an immense dry lake bed for emergency landing purposes. The extremely hard, flat, forty-four-square-mile expanse of Rogers Dry Lake made it the perfect place to land high-performance experimental aircraft. And, in the years since the first flight of the XP-59A, the Army Air Forces had shifted an ever-increasing volume of its flight testing activities from Wright Field, in Ohio, to the remote Mojave Desert installation. Thus, in addition to unsurpassed natural advantages, the base was configured to provide at least the minimum levels of support that would be required to conduct an experimental flight test program.

Jack Russell In New York, we proceeded to get our part of the job done. After that, my crew and I left Buffalo and headed for Muroc to meet the airplane when it was sent out. Once we were in California we traveled through more desert and more desert all the way until we got near the north lake bed. There were no paved roads into the base at all from the north at that time. There was just a sand road off of Highway 58 that the guy who was driving knew about. We went across that little sandy stretch of road and dropped down onto the lake bed, and there he stopped to let everybody take a look. You could see mirages all over the place, like we were driving into water, and the buildings were all waving around. He said, "That's where you're going to live, down there where you see that big lump of dark

An aerial view of Muroc Army Air Field in October 1946. The vast stretches of Rogers Dry Lake, seen to the right just off the end of the runway, gave many a worried test pilot plenty of room to bring in a crippled airplane. Today this base is called Edwards Air Force Base, and it still provides an advantageous spot for flight testing, and for landing the Space Shuttles.

Bell Aircraft prepared two XS-1 planes—serial numbers 6062 and 6063. The 6062 was the number one XS-1, and 6063 was the number two XS-1, used by NACA as its test vehicle. The number two XS-1 was first flown in September 1947. The sound barrier was broken by 6062.

stuff." One of the guys said, "Would you turn this car around and take me back to Barstow? I'd like to go home!" Another said, "We're going to live there?" The driver said, "Oh, it'll be all right when we get closer." So we drove across the lake bed and soon we saw the barracks and the hangar that we were going to occupy. The barracks building was not even finished. A lot of the windows were not in place yet. The sand storms out there were just terrible at the time, so the place would be full of sand—on the floor, in the bed. Of course, we worked so many hours we weren't in our rooms very much.

The food there wasn't all that good. There were a lot of complaints about the food from everybody. One day the acting chief test pilot at the base said, "Well, I've made arrangements, and we're all going to go down to the Army Mess in the morning for breakfast." So he got a big truck; we all piled in the back and he

Even the high and mighty were brought low by Muroc's humble facilities. Here Larry Bell, president of Bell Aircraft, sits on his bunk at the "Desert Rat" Hotel.

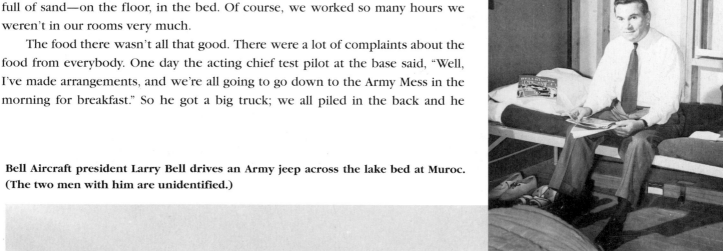

Bell Aircraft president Larry Bell drives an Army jeep across the lake bed at Muroc. (The two men with him are unidentified.)

drove us all the way down to the other end of the base, five or six miles. That food there was worse than ours! The next morning he was out front honking the horn, waiting to go down there again, and nobody came out! The food did get a little better the more we complained. They tried to bring in better cooks and it became fairly livable after that.

Part of the problem was that the cooking crews kept quitting. We finally found out why. It seems that every time the cooks went out the back door to dump the trash, they'd run into a rattlesnake. They were in the hangar, so it wasn't anything new to us, but the cooks would just pack their suitcases and leave once they saw a

Muroc Army Air Field, now Edwards Air Force Base, is a near-perfect environment for test flying. The weather rarely interferes with test flight schedules, and the dry lake beds offer many square miles of flat, unobstructed landing area. Landings of the XS-1 were uneventful as long as the fuel was jettisoned beforehand. The XS-1 landing gear was not designed to handle the extra weight of fuel.

rattlesnake. So we kept changing personnel all the time. It was kind of exciting because every once in a while somebody in the hangar would holler, "There's a snake in the front door!" We had .22 rifles and everybody was scared to death that somebody was going to get accidentally shot out there, because everyone was trying to kill a little snake. The snakes gradually gave way to us, but between them and jackrabbits and coyotes, we had a lot of animals running around.

Chapter Four

The Air Force Takes Over the XS-1 Program

James Young Meanwhile, back at Buffalo, Bell personnel completed checkouts of the second (number two) XS-1 in preparation for its ferry flight aboard the B-29 carrier aircraft to Muroc. The first (number one) aircraft, with its thin, 8-percent wing, was still undergoing engine installation and, thus, the number two vehicle would be the first to fly at Muroc. It arrived during the second week of October and successfully completed its first unpowered checkout flight on October 11. Three more glide flights followed, all of which were uneventful.

By the end of February 1947, Slick Goodlin, who had been sent to Muroc by Bell to continue as test pilot, had completed twelve powered flights in the number two aircraft. He succeeded in fulfilling Bell's contractual requirements by attaining a top speed of Mach 0.82. He had also demonstrated the structural ruggedness of the craft by completing 8.7G pullups at speeds ranging from 0.4 to 0.8 Mach.

In order to fulfill all of its requirements, however, the Bell Company had to complete a total of twenty powered flights, including at least five flights in each of the two airplanes. The number one aircraft, with its thin 8-percent wing and 6-percent tail, arrived at Muroc in early April, and after a single glide flight, Goodlin completed its first powered flight on April 11. Between that date and May 29, the number one aircraft completed six more flights, and the number two vehicle was launched two more times, bringing Bell's demonstration of airworthiness to a very satisfactory conclusion.

Bell's hopes of completing the U.S. Army Air Forces' accelerated research program had long since faded by that time. In the postwar drawdown, research and development budgets had been slashed to the bone. Stated simply, the Air Materiel Command (AMC) did not have the funding to support a contract with Bell to conduct the program. Moreover, AMC officials were adamantly opposed to paying the exorbitant amount—$150,000, payable over five years—that Slick Goodlin was

The XS-1 flew its early missions with no power. But these glide flights were useful in determining the aerodynamic characteristics of the airplane and in giving the pilot a feel for the controls, the visibility, and the landing patterns on Rogers Dry Lake. All flights on the X-1 ended with dead-stick landings, since all fuel was routinely jettisoned prior to touchdown. The thirteen-mile-long lake bed gave the pilots a huge margin of error. Even so, the runout on an XS-1 landing was about three miles. Here, the number two aircraft (6063) makes a landing.

Walt Williams, chief of the National Advisory Committee for Aeronautics' XS-1 test team at Muroc, stands at the podium at a NACA gathering, probably after the breaking of the sound barrier. Seated to his left is pilot Chuck Yeager. At far right is crew chief Jack Russell. Williams's team had been deployed to Muroc from Langley Field in Virginia in a research-gathering and oversight capacity. They did not always see eye to eye with the "hell bent for leather" Air Force team.

Gen. Albert G. Boyd.

Chuck Yeager in 1948.

reportedly demanding to complete the program when they could get one of their own test pilots to fly it for a standard monthly salary.

Not long after a March 6 conference with Bell and NACA officials, Col. George F. Smith, chief of the Air Projects Section of the Army Materiel Command, simply called Col. Albert Boyd, the indomitable chief of the Flight Test Division at Wright Field, and asked him if his people could conduct the accelerated test program. Enthusiastically, he replied, "You bet!" Boyd was eager to prove that the military—and especially his test pilots—could successfully conduct experimental research programs.

Boyd, who has justifiably been called the "father" of modern Air Force testing, had served as chief of the Flight Test Division since 1945. Under his stern glare, only the very best pilots—those who convincingly demonstrated their discipline, objectivity, precision flying skills, and love for the job—were permitted to fly tests. The rest were unceremoniously weeded out. Thus Boyd was building a cadre of top-notch test pilots. He was trying to professionalize the art and science of test flying within the AAF. He was also one of the first to recognize that, in this new era of high-speed flight with complex new machines and the proliferation of sophisticated onboard systems, test pilots were going to have to be more than just good "stick-and-rudder men"; they were also going to have to have a solid engineering background. By 1946, he had already begun to build his cadre of professionals and he was just waiting for the opportunity for them to prove their worth. The X-1 program seemed to offer the best of all possible opportunities.

By May, Colonel Boyd was confident enough that the Flight Test Division would be selected for the accelerated research program of the XS-1 that they began the selection process for the AMC crew that would be responsible for flying the airplane. As chief of the division, he had the ultimate responsibility for making the choice from a long list of volunteers. Boyd wanted a pilot with extremely precise—or "scientific"—flying capabilities and, above all, one who was "rock-solid in stability." As he agonized over the selection, he kept coming back to a very junior test pilot, Capt. Charles E. Yeager. Though he lacked a college education, Boyd considered him the best instinctive pilot he had ever seen. Ultimately, this was the decisive factor. Yeager was selected to be the primary XS-1 pilot.

Chuck Yeager In the spring of 1947, Col. Al Boyd, then chief of the Flight Test Division at Wright Field, reacted favorably to Air Materiel Command's proposal that the Air Force take over the XS-1 program. He had previously argued that the Air Force had pilots who were as well qualified as the Bell civilian test pilots, and that the program was being seriously delayed because of the hassle between Slick Goodlin and Bell. Air Force pilots, he said, would not negotiate fees; they flew because it was their job. The AMC agreed, and the Air Force stepped in and took over the XS-1 program.

Colonel Boyd personally screened most of the pilots in the Flight Test Division. As he began to evaluate pilots for the XS-1 program, he narrowed the field down to fighter pilots, because flying the XS-1 fit into their single-engine, single-cockpit mentality. He looked mostly to the fighter pilots in the Fighter Test Section of the Flight Test Division. As luck would have it, Colonel Boyd finally picked me as the

Test pilot, Cal Tech graduate, and master of working aerodynamics, Jackie Ridley was a natural liaison between the scientists and the pilots in the X-1 program. He is widely acknowledged as the originator of the flying tail concept that enabled the XS-1 to break the sound barrier.

primary pilot, and Lt. Bob Hoover as my backup pilot. In talking with General Boyd later, I learned the reason he picked me specifically was because of my stability and performance in previous tests, plus the fact that I had a background in aircraft maintenance, understood machinery, and never had too much trouble keeping an aircraft flying. In short, he liked the way I flew. Although I did not have a great education and was not a West Pointer, as some of the officers in the Flight Test Division would have preferred for the XS-1, I still had a great deal of experience in combat, in maintenance, and in running functional test flights on aircraft. Also, in the spring of 1946 I had been selected to go to the Test Pilot School at Wright Field, where I had done quite well.

James Young First Lt. Robert A. "Bob" Hoover, another pilot with exceptional skills, was chosen as the backup pilot. Capt. Jackie L. Ridley, a young test pilot with an M.S. in aeronautical engineering from the California Institute of Technology, was assigned as the project engineer. Boyd believed that Ridley, with his background in test flying and his unique ability to translate esoteric concepts into everyday terms, would be able to provide the pilots with all of the engineering expertise they would need.

Bob Hoover I was absolutely convinced from the first time I got exposed to the program that it would be successful. The big concern up until that program was whether or not an airplane could stand the forces that would be exerted upon it as you exceeded the speed of sound. Jackie Ridley and others convinced me that the airplane was designed for more Gs than a human being could accept, and therefore, the airplane would hold together.

My positive feelings about the program were enhanced by my conversations with some of the German scientists who were in camp at Wright Field. Captured during the war, they were brought over so we could gain as much knowledge from them as we could. They had built the Me-163, which was their experimental rocket-powered airplane. They gained a lot of experience with that airplane, but they also had a lot of fatalities. It burned highly exotic fuel and frequently it would get out of control and explode. I recall one pilot who had landed and flipped upside down in rough terrain with some residual fuel on board. When we went out there to recover the pilot, he was literally dissolved. There was nothing there but a skeleton. The fuels were that volatile. It was a treacherous airplane, but it did have enormous capability.

James Young The day after the go-ahead for the Flight Test Division to proceed with the program, key personnel from the Flight Test Division and the Aircraft Projects Section of the Engineering Division met to discuss the AMC program and how it would interact with the NACA test program. The Flight Test Division's program would parallel NACA's program, but, avoiding duplication wherever possible, it would proceed at a much more accelerated pace, and its goal would be to attain a Mach number of 1.1 in the shortest possible time.

To facilitate this effort, the Flight Test Division wanted to employ the number

OPPOSITE AND OVERLEAF: **Test pilot Bob Hoover was Yeager's backup pilot in the XS-1 program, and flew high chase for most XS-1 flights. Although he never got to fly the XS-1, he had a long career test flying for North American and is considered the finest aerobatic pilot in the world.**

Test pilots look over the Bell XS-1 in 1947. Chuck Yeager is second from left; Chalmers H. "Slick" Goodlin, who was a civilian test pilot for Bell and who replaced Jack Woolams in the X-1 cockpit, is third from the right.

one aircraft with its thinner wings and tail. Its higher speed capabilities were obviously more compatible with the Army Air Forces' immediate Mach 1.0 objective, while the number two vehicle, with its thicker airfoils, would have a lower critical Mach number and, hence, would be better suited to NACA's desire to systematically collect detailed transonic data. This would be the Army Air Forces' first foray into experimental research flying and, while not wishing to go it alone, the Flight Test Division wanted to have as many of its own personnel involved as was practicable. Thus it insisted that its own crew should fly the B-29 launch aircraft for all of the accelerated tests with the number one XS-1. It also wanted to provide its own maintenance crew for the B-29 and at least four personnel to assist in the maintenance and servicing of the XS-1. Further, while the Flight Test Division agreed that responsibility for instrumentation and telemetry should be in the hands of NACA, it also wanted its people involved in these activities. It was obvious that, by these means, the military organization was hoping to gain the type of knowledge that would permit it to expand its role in any future experimental programs. The XS-1 program would be more than just an attempt to achieve a major milestone in aviation; it would also be an invaluable learning experience upon which to base a nascent military flight research capability.

Chapter Five

The X-1 Team Assembles at Muroc

James Young After a quick trip to the Bell facility in Buffalo to get their first close-up look at one of the X-1s and its XLR-11 engine, Yeager, Hoover, and Ridley proceeded to Muroc in late July. Maj. Robert L. "Bob" Cardenas, an experienced multiengine test pilot, had been selected as administrative officer in charge of the AMC-X1 test unit at Muroc. He would also pilot the B-29 launch aircraft with Lt. Edward L. Swindell serving as his flight engineer. By July 27, the whole team had assembled at Muroc and was in the process of establishing office and maintenance facilities.

Robert Cardenas Albert Boyd had a genius in being able to read people and to pick the right person for a job. He chose Chuck as the pilot of the X-1 not only because of his ability as a pilot, which he had proven in World War II as a leading ace, but also because of Chuck's natural ability with machines. Chuck had a mechanic's touch. Boyd chose Bob Hoover, who was a great stick-and-rudder man, to be the alternate in case anything happened to Chuck. Jackie Ridley was chosen for his engineering ability, but above all for his ability to communicate with Chuck. They understood each other and talked easily. Dick Frost was brought in from Bell Aircraft. Dick had been living with the airplane from the drawing board on, and he was also a test pilot. Dick would pass to Jackie the total knowledge he had of the airplane, which Jackie would then communicate to Chuck. We also had Jack Russell, a very important fellow. He was the crew chief on the X-1 and the only one who had really worked with the rocket motors before. My job was purely and simply to run the team. I did not think too much about it at the time, but now I can hardly imagine trying to control Chuck Yeager, Bob Hoover, and Jackie Ridley all at the same time. I was the administrative officer in charge of the project, and the B-29 pilot who had to drop Chuck on time, on schedule. Boyd's genius was in getting the right people together, then leaving them alone until they got the job done. And he did.

All of the Mach One team pilots assembled for this photograph in 1947. *Front row, left to right:* Bob Cardenas, Chuck Yeager, and Jackie Ridley. *In the back, left to right:* Bob Hoover and Dick Frost.

Maj. Bob Cardenas stands in front of a captured German jet-powered bomber at Wright Field. Cardenas was a top multiengine pilot and was the Air Force's chief test pilot on the YB-49 "flying wing" bomber.

Dick Frost was a test pilot for Bell Aircraft who served as project engineer for Bell not only on the X-1 but also on the X-1A, X-1B, and X-1D programs. He also flew low chase on flying days for the X-1. Here he straps into his parachute harness prior to a test flight at the Bell plant in Niagara Falls, New York.

Jack Russell General Boyd picked what is now known as the Mach One pilot team—Yeager, Hoover, and Ridley. I knew them all well. Yeager had quite an exemplary flying record. I knew he was a little hard to tame, though, and it was tough to get him to do what was necessary, rather than just to fly the airplane upside down all the time. I'd flown with him before and we were never right side up. I said to him, "Don't you ever fly with the cockpit up on the top?" He'd say, "Not if I can help it." But he was one of those people who just loved flying and did everything very, very well. He was the type of guy who would risk his neck on almost

Crew Chief Jack Russell works on the X-1s in the refueling area in September 1947.

INSET: The four-chamber, 6,000-pound-thrust XLR-11 rocket engine gets a ground test.

BELOW: The X-1's rocket engines are firing in a ground test, and the noise level is so high that crewmen have to hold their ears.

Flight test engineer Jackie Ridley walks in front of the B-29 as it is towed into takeoff position. Ridley was killed in an aviation accident in 1957. The Ridley Mission Control Center at Edwards Air Force Base, California, is named in his honor.

anything. Jackie Ridley was one of the top engineers around and the most easy-going of the bunch. He really knew his engineering and Yeager relied on everything Ridley said. Bob Cardenas was the pilot for the B-29 and also was very involved in meetings about the whole program. He didn't hang around with us in the hangar, so I never really got too well acquainted with him, at least not in the same way as I did with Yeager and Ridley. But Bob was always a very pleasant guy, and we got along well; everybody liked him.

And let's not forget Dick Frost, the project engineer of the airplane with Bell Aircraft. Dick knew every facet of the airplane, was a pilot himself, and was a wonderful guy. His help was invaluable to the program.

The number two X-1 is shown in the maintenance area of Muroc. The various wiring harnesses and control cables can be seen with the fuselage skin removed.

Jackie Ridley and Chuck Yeager (*standing, second and third from left*) with members of the ground crew, including (*left to right, front row*) **Merle Woods, Jack Russell, and Garth Dill.**

Chuck Yeager Bob Hoover and I devoted all of our time to learning the systems on the XS-1, which by now we just called the X-1. Bell Aircraft Corporation had given the Air Force Jack Russell, the crew chief on the X-1, letting the Air Force hire him as civil service personnel. This allowed for a great deal of continuity in the maintenance program of the X-1. Jack knew the X-1 inside and out. They also gave us Dick Frost, who was a Bell test pilot and knew more about the X-1, both from maintenance and in-flight-test point of view, than any other single individual.

Col. Albert Boyd added Capt. Jack Ridley as the flight test engineer on the program. Jack had his master's degree from Cal Tech and had studied under Dr. Theodor von Kármán, a well-known aeronautical engineer. Jack was very intelligent and a very good test pilot. He added a huge element of communication between me and NACA, which was involved in the program to receive flight test data (having installed the instrumentation in the X-1). Jack also consulted with the Air Force on its goal of advancing the speed of the aircraft.

I went to Muroc in August of 1947 with the X-1, and I spent a great deal of time there learning the systems.

Early-morning operations at the fueling area on the far west end of the Muroc flight line. Chuck Yeager inspects the cockpit.

The rocket engines on the number two X-1 are tested just prior to the airplane's first flight, on September 25, 1947. Although this airplane was NACA's test aircraft, there were no NACA pilots checked out on it, so Chuck Yeager completed the flight for NACA.

INSET: A close view of the X-1's rocket engine and the configuration of its four chambers.

One of the few color photographs taken during the X-1 project was this early-morning shot of pilot Chuck Yeager and the burnt orange X-1. This photo was taken by Jackie Ridley. Ridley's shadow can be seen to the immediate left of Yeager.

INSET: *Glamorous Glen* was the name Chuck Yeager gave to his P-51 fighter aircraft in World War II. He continued the tradition, with *Glamorous Glennis,* for a number of X-1 airplanes, including the plane in which he made his momentous flight.

Chapter Six

The Happy Bottom Riding Club

James Young To relieve the stress of test flying, and to find some fun out in the desert, the pilots and contractors assigned to Muroc would frequent a ranch near the base called Rancho Oro Verde Fly Inn Dude Ranch, better known to history as the Happy Bottom Riding Club. It was owned and run by Pancho Barnes [her birth name was Florence Lowe], a famous aviatrix who had started flying back in the barnstormer days. Pancho's ranch was the recreational sanctuary for the test pilots at Muroc. It was at Pancho's place where the guys would go to celebrate their victories and sometimes to mourn their losses. It was at Pancho's where they would sit at the bar over drinks to talk shop and certainly to relieve a great deal of the stress under which they lived. These guys were flying constantly, and it is hard for us to conceive of the kinds of schedules they maintained. They were in and out of cockpits. The desire to get the airplanes tested and move on was very intense. It was a very accelerated kind of environment and the flying was very dangerous. They were constantly living with the knowledge that the next time they flew their number could come up. Pancho gave these guys a place to go where they could let off steam and commiserate with each other.

Bob Hoover Muroc was a grim place in those years. It was desolate, and when the wind would blow, it would blow strong. It was dusty and uncomfortable and you felt isolated. There wasn't much to do. We'd fly when we had something to fly, or hang around the engineering offices. We flew other airplanes as well as being assigned to the X-1 program. Chuck and I flew a lot of F-84s; as a matter of fact, we associated with the first F-84 fighter group. They trained at the North Base and we had a chance to visit with them frequently. It made for a lot of fun at the officer's club because it was pretty quiet there with only Chuck and me and a handful of others. With all those fighter pilots there, we had some fun.

Florence Lowe "Pancho" Barnes was a legendary pilot and character in the aviation community and a fixture on the scene at Muroc in the 1940s and 1950s. The daughter of wealthy parents, she was raised in luxury in southern California and had many Hollywood friends. Her spirit was Rabelaisian, and she pursued her maverick love of flying to a ranch and airfield in the desert near Muroc Army Air Field, later Edwards Air Force Base, where she flew her airplanes and entertained her friends, among them the "right stuff" test pilots.

Pancho Barnes was an accomplished aviatrix. She was a barnstormer and stunt pilot, and at one point took the women's air speed record from Amelia Earhart. Here she poses with her crew in the late 1920s.

Robert Cardenas A lot of people forget that the Happy Bottom Riding Club was Pancho's home. She really did not operate the place for profit. And if you were there, it was because you had been invited there. You were a guest in her home even if you may have paid for your drinks and meals now and then. When she wanted to celebrate something she managed the guest list. She knew who was going to be there. You might drop in on Pancho Barnes, but you would not be allowed to stay if she did not want you to stay.

If there had not been a Pancho or a ranch, all the events leading up to breaking the sound barrier would have been much more difficult. The guys needed a place to relax, to let of steam, because things could get tense now and then. While she did not have anything directly to do with breaking the sound barrier, we were glad she was there. We could have gone to Lancaster or Antelope Valley or even to Beverly Hills, but Pancho's was right across the road and it was where we wanted to be. She had a swimming pool. The food was not gourmet, but it was darn good—steaks and fries and so on. The drinks were reasonably priced—whenever they were priced. And then she had young ladies who worked there that had gone to Hollywood to become stars and did not quite make it. They were there to play the piano, sing, and dance with the guests. It was a good place to have good food and good fun.

The gatherings at Pancho's were always lively, like this night around the piano. With Pancho are famous pilots (_clockwise from the piano player_) Gus Askounis, Jackie Ridley, Ike Northrop, "Pete" Everest, Chuck Yeager, and Bud Anderson.

At one point, Pancho decided to make her place (then called the Rancho Oro Verde) a private club, and she issued membership cards to her favorites. Pilot Bob Hoover remembers that he and Chuck Yeager were members two and one, respectively. This card belonged to Cliff "Snuffy" Morris, who worked for the National Advisory Committee for Aeronautics.

No. 276

PANCHO'S RANCHO ORO VERDE
MUROC, CALIFORNIA
CO-OP CLUB
MEMBER
Happy Bottom Riding Club

Cliff Morris

ISSUED 9-1-47   EXPIRES 9-1-48

Pancho Barnes   ISSUED BY PCB

Bob Hoover I first met Pancho when Chuck and I went over for a visit. It was my first time there but he had been there before. She took me in immediately and treated me with great friendliness and introduced me to a lot of people. She was down-to-earth and very generous to both of us. That doesn't mean she didn't charge us occasionally, but it never seemed to matter whether she got paid or not, she just enjoyed being with you.

I was sitting there one night and Pancho wanted to know why I was just a first lieutenant. I explained my story to her, and she said, "Well, I can take care of that." So, she picked up the phone and called Washington and got Gen. Tooey Spaatz on the phone and I just about panicked. Can you imagine waking up the top commanding general at three o'clock in the morning? She was reading him the riot act: "Tooey, you gotta do somethin' about this and I wanna hear from you tomorrow about it!" I'm sure he just placated her with "Sure, sure, sure." I kept saying, "Don't mention my name, don't mention my name!" Nothing ever came of it, so he probably went back to sleep and said, "Well, that's my friend Pancho." That was the end of it, but I was sure worried. I thought, "Boy, I'll never get promoted now."

The amenities of life at Muroc were few and far between in the years after World War II. This was Ma Greene's Cafe, near a part of Muroc called Kerosene Flats. If you weren't at Pancho's, you were here.

George Hurrell photo of Pancho taken before the first women's Transcontinental Air Derby in 1929. Pancho was an accomplished air racer and formed lifelong friendships with fellow air racers Jimmy Doolittle, Hap Arnold, and Tooey Spaatz.

World War II pilot Eugene "Mac" McKendry married Pancho Barnes at the Happy Bottom Riding Club. At the wedding, Chuck Yeager gave away the bride. Al Boyd served as best man.

Mac McKendry, Pancho's husband She had fixed up the ranch very much like a Mexican hacienda. She wanted all the buildings to seem as though they were built out of stone, but she used cement, with rough edges all around. Her house was initially the central point of the ranch, which grew over time. The first bar was only about fifty feet from our bedroom. The dance hall and later the motel were built not very far away. The motel was U-shaped by the time it was all completed. In the front were the offices and a large archway that went up three stories, with a mission design. Of course, we had to put a flashing red light up there so the planes wouldn't run into it at night. The airport was a quarter mile away, and we would drive over to bring our guests in. We had air-conditioning and our own heat in each room. I don't think anyone else in the Antelope Valley had that in 1946.

People have said that Pancho's was a bordello, but that was not true and was put forward by the people that got tossed out, because you couldn't get away with it. The Alcoholic Beverage Control, which handled the liquor licenses, were extremely strict in those days. They'd have taken our license on sight with anything like that going on.

Pancho knew that military people were paid very little money compared to everybody else. The civilian contractors were making so much more money than the military pilots that Pancho felt that it was unfair. So anybody in the military, and of course even any other pilots that she knew anywhere that had problems, she was always willing to help. She'd offer them money, or a place to stay, or feed them until they would get on their feet again. She always had a warm spot for the military guys.

Perhaps the most important man in aviation after World War II was Larry Bell, president of the Bell Aircraft Corporation. The X-1 aircraft was a Bell company design, and Bell understood the economic importance of supersonic capability for his company. Like everyone else, he conducted a lot of work and play at Pancho's, as here in the summer of 1947.

Robert Cardenas Pancho was a remarkable woman. There were many Panchos, not just one. She could fly the hell out of an airplane. She ran a ranch that she was proud of. Privately, when she was in Beverly Hills, she was a different person. She had many powerful, wealthy friends, including Hap Arnold, Tooey Spaatz, and Jimmy Doolittle. They knew her from way back when. Then there was the Pancho who was with the pilots. She could talk airplanes, which endeared her to us. She could also outcuss any mule skinner out there in the desert. She was good-hearted, she was one of us, and she took care of us. We felt comfortable with her. We could tell her anything; we could cry on her shoulder if we wanted to. She was a settling influence, and I would always like to remember her the way she was, in flying boots and breeches. We had a ball out there in the desert with her. She left her mark on Muroc and she is a part of aviation history.

RIGHT AND OPPOSITE: **Pancho Barnes's ranch went by various names over the course of ten years, but it was always called "Pancho's." She was a born party hostess, with a ribald sense of humor. Her bar-restaurant became the "fraternity house" for test pilots, engineers, and aviation executives who needed a place to blow off steam. Her place was as well known in the aviation community as Muroc itself, and became the sentimental heart of the period known now as the golden age of test flight.**

Pancho's connections with the Hollywood crowd and the proximity of her ranch to Los Angeles often brought film crews who needed a desert or Western location for their films. Here, in the late 1940s, actress Shelley Winters takes a break from shooting near Pancho's to say hello to an appreciative group of test pilots. They are (*left to right*) Jackie Ridley; Jimmy Doolittle, Jr.; Chuck Yeager; Col. Leonard Wiehrdt; and Pete Everest.

Pancho Barnes had been born into one of California's wealthiest families and grew up surrounded by Hollywood celebrities of the 1930s, 1940s, and 1950s. After she moved to the desert to fly her beloved airplanes, her Hollywood friends would often come for visits. Many of them were pilots themselves. Here, in 1948, Pancho is flanked by Roy Rogers and Carl Bellinger, a test pilot. John Payne, Robert Taylor, Errol Flynn, Dick Powell, Veronica Lake, Nicky Hilton and his then-girlfriend Elizabeth Taylor, and Edgar Bergen were among those who either had their own airplanes and flew to Pancho's or drove out from Los Angeles.

The bar at Pancho Barnes's Happy Bottom Riding Club was the one place near Muroc Army Air Field in the late 1940s where pilots, engineers, aviation executives, and Air Force brass could unwind, have a few drinks, talk about airplanes, and forget how godforsaken a place Muroc was to live and work in. It was in this bar that engineers drew wing designs on cocktail napkins, where hot-shot pilots were recruited to test fly for ambitious airplane companies, and where the young men with the right stuff celebrated their victories and toasted the dead. If this period in aviation history was the golden age of flight, then Pancho's place was its headquarters.

Dr. Barney Oldfield (*far right*) enjoyed Pancho's immensely and celebrated one of his wedding anniversaries there. The gathering included the usual suspects and Pancho, who is seated next to General Shoop.

Four legendary names in American aviation hoot it up at Pancho's—Chuck Yeager, Jackie Ridley, Pancho Barnes, and Pete Everest. Pancho was a "gold mine" of information about early air racing and stunt flying to these young test pilots. According to Mac McKendry, "Pancho loved Chuck Yeager, and if any other test pilot dared to criticize Yeager in her presence, Pancho would have me throw them out of the bar!"

A dinner party at Pancho's included the superstars of American aviation and some of their wives.

CLOCKWISE STARTING AT FAR LEFT: Anna Lou Boyd, Al Boyd, Ellie Anderson, Bud Anderson, Glennis Yeager, Chuck Yeager, unknown, Peter Everest, Gus Askounis, Stoney Knight, Ike Northrop, Nell Ridley, Jackie Ridley.

Base commander Gen. Albert Boyd and his wife, Anna Lou, pose with a true Hollywood star—the dog Lassie—at Pancho's.

Life on the base at Muroc was tough for the families of test pilots. In addition to the normal anxiety about the dangers of test flying, families had to endure the base's spartan living conditions and the desert heat. But Glennis Yeager and the children handled it well. From left, Chuck, Susie, Donnie, Mike, Glennis, and Sharon.

When the pilots weren't flying, there was other fun to be had at Pancho's ranch. It was a good place to hunt, and she let some of her favorites shoot jackrabbits whenever they wanted. Here, Pete Everest (*far right*), Chuck Yeager (*second from right*), and Gen. Al Boyd (*center, with rifle*) show off a day's work.

ABOVE AND RIGHT: **Pancho's Rancho Oro Verde had the look and feel of a desert hacienda, and included a motel, with a fountain in the courtyard shaped like the Army Air Corps emblem.**

An aerial view of Pancho's 360-acre ranch, which sat just beyond the main runway at Muroc. Many of Pancho's aviator friends liked to "buzz" the house on takeoff, getting their wheels so low that they grazed the building.

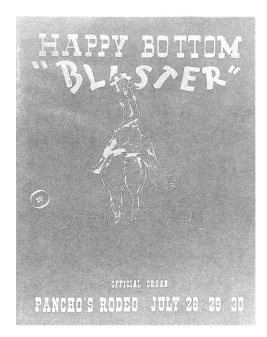

The rodeos at Pancho's were partly staged for fun, but this was real cowboy country, and the bronc-riding and calf-roping contests featured the valley's working cowboys. There was real prize money offered, and Pancho even built grandstands, thinking that regular rodeos would be a big source of revenue. They weren't.

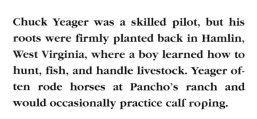

Chuck Yeager was a skilled pilot, but his roots were firmly planted back in Hamlin, West Virginia, where a boy learned how to hunt, fish, and handle livestock. Yeager often rode horses at Pancho's ranch and would occasionally practice calf roping.

Pancho Barnes (*center*) with the pilots who made up the first Motion Picture Stunt Pilots Association, a group she founded after arguments about safety and pay with film studio mogul Howard Hughes.

In 1948 Pancho Barnes got the Motion Picture Stunt Pilots Association to honor Chuck Yeager with an honorary membership for breaking the sound barrier. The celebration was at the Hollywood Roosevelt Hotel. Notables in the group included Pancho (*on the floor, at right*), Yeager (*in plaid suit, standing next to the trophy*), and a young man whom Pancho taught to fly at her civilian pilot training school at her ranch in 1941–42, Kirk Kirkorian (*back row, second from left*). Kirkorian later parlayed that experience into hundreds of millions of dollars in the aviation industry, as the owner of TransWorld Airlines (TWA).

On November 14, 1953, the Air Force and Pancho Barnes finally came to blows when the service wanted to extend its new 15,000-foot runway through Pancho's ranch. The Air Force called it an obstruction in the clearway and wanted it razed. She put up a fight, but before the matter could be resolved in court, the ranch mysteriously burned to the ground. Although arson was suspected, no charges were ever filed. This event marked the end of an era. While the flight test operations at Edwards increased over the years, nothing ever replaced the Happy Bottom Riding Club nor approached its legendary status as the home of the Supersonic Pilots Club.

Chapter Seven

Powered Flight Testing

James Young The X-1 program began with "familiarization schooling" for Yeager, Hoover, and Ridley. For four days Dick Frost tried to teach them everything he knew about the X-1. The ground school was completed by August 1, and the test team turned toward preparations for Yeager's first unpowered familiarization flight.

Installation of the engine was delayed because of a shortage of parts and thus the XS-1 carried ballast instead of an engine when Yeager finally entered the cockpit for his first flight on August 6. At 18,000 feet, he dropped from the darkness of the B-29's bomb bay into the blinding sunlight and, almost without thinking, performed a brief series of slow rolls. Gliding downward, he later recalled that the X-1 was "graceful, responsive, and beautiful to handle." The whole eight-minute flight, all the way to touchdown and rollout on Rogers Dry Lake, went flawlessly and, from Yeager's point of view, almost effortlessly. The same was true of his second flight the next day, and during his final glide flight on August 8, he actually engaged Bob Hoover in his chase P-80 in a mock dogfight as they spiraled downward. These three brief flights left Yeager with a high level of confidence concerning his ability to fly the airplane; he felt more than ready to begin the powered-flight program.

Chuck Yeager Like Jack Woolams before me, my first flights in the X-1 were not powered flights. I made three glide flights without any propellants in the aircraft in order to get the handling characteristics and a feel for the aircraft on landing. On the glide flights, Bob Hoover chased me in an FP-80, and Dick Frost would fly either a P-51 or FP-80 chase aircraft (FP-80s were faster photo reconnaissance versions of the P-80 "Shooting Star"). After three glide flights, I felt comfortable in the aircraft. It flew very nice and quiet, the controls were good, and system coordination was good.

James Young Unfortunately, the team would have to wait three weeks for a powered flight. A shortage of parts and tools continued to delay installation of the engine so that ground tests of the engine-installed aircraft did not get under way

The Bell XS-1, with its orange paint, glows in the desert sun as it sits on the ramp at Muroc. The engineer in the cockpit demonstrates the close quarters up front.

until August 27. Two days later, Yeager's wait was finally over, as the B-29 carried the burnt orange–colored rocket plane aloft for the first powered flight in the accelerated program. As the bomber climbed through 7,000 feet, Yeager slipped into the cockpit. Chilled to the bone by the liquid oxygen (LOX) stored in the tank directly behind the cockpit, he completed all of his preflight checklist procedures. After Cardenas piloted the aircraft to about 25,000 feet, he nosed the B-29 over into a shallow dive. At 21,000 feet and a speed of 255 mph, the X-1 was released. Approximately ten seconds later, Yeager ignited the first chamber of his engine and was slammed back in his seat. After five seconds, he ignited the number two chamber while shutting down chamber number one. Repeating this procedure for each of the rocket chambers, he executed a slow roll at one point, and when the craft attained zero G, the engine shut down because of a drop in LOX tank pressure. He successfully relit the engine and, rocketing upward at 0.7 Mach, finally leveled off at about 45,000 feet.

After shutting off the engine, he rolled over into a dive and sped downward. Ultimately attaining a top speed of approximately 0.8 Mach during his unpowered descent, he recovered from the dive at about 5,000 feet. At this point, he ignited chamber number one and initiated a shallow climb. Then, in rapid sequence, he lit the remaining chambers. As he later recalled, "the impact nearly knocks you back into last week. That nose is pointed so straight up that you can't see the blue sky out the windshield! We are no longer an airplane: We're a skyrocket. You're not flying. You're holding on to a tiger's tail. Straight up, you're going .75 Mach! In one minute the fuel is gone. By then you're at 35,000 feet, traveling at .85 Mach. You're so excited, scared, and thrilled that you can't say a word until the next day."

But, as he recalled, "others said plenty." The flight plan had stipulated that he should not exceed Mach 0.82 on this flight, and as a professional test pilot, he was expected to abide by its requirements. The NACA team questioned Yeager's sense of discipline. His sternest critic, however, was Colonel Boyd, who "fired a rocket of his own." He was not about to see the program jeopardized by a reckless disregard for discipline. "Reply by endorsement," he wrote, "about why you exceeded .82 Mach in violation of my direct orders." Yeager replied that any deviations were "due to the excited condition of the undersigned," and he assured Colonel Boyd that the AMC test team considered safety-related matters to be of utmost importance.

Chuck Yeager A few days after my glide flights, we started our first powered flights. Prior to the flight we had a meeting with NACA's Walt Williams, Dee Beeler, and some of the instrumentation people, with Jack Ridley, Bob Hoover, Dick Frost, and me. We talked about what we were going to do on the first powered flight and came up with an "aim-for" Mach number. I figured we might as well aim for .82 Mach if we had no indication of a problem. So, on the first powered flight, after the drop from the B-29 at around 24,000 feet, I fired one chamber; then fired off the second chamber and turned off the first; fired the third chamber, turned off the second; fired the fourth chamber and turned off the third; a procedure that showed me all my chambers were operating. I pulled up and did a roll with the aircraft. When I pulled the nose up and did the roll, I decreased the Gs to about zero. This

The X-1 was towed by tractor to the fueling area prior to test flights. In the foreground is the pit into which the plane was lowered to facilitate shackling onto the B-29 bomb bay.

caused the rocket engine to stop running. I could not figure out why until later when I got on the ground and found that the liquid oxygen in the fuel tank was cavitating [creating partial vacuums in the flowing liquid] when I went to zero G. That, of course, would interrupt the flow of liquid oxygen to the rocket engine and we would get a flameout. But once I rolled out again, the chamber would reignite. I shut off the rocket engine, came down at 450 mph in a steep dive across the field, and pulled up and ignited all four chambers. The airplane really took off. I got up to .8 Mach very quickly. In order to keep the aircraft below .82, which was our Mach number aim, I pulled the airplane up into a vertical climb. I was doing a modified barrel roll going straight up. But as I went through 38–40,000 feet, and dropped the nose a little bit, the first thing I knew I was up to .84 Mach number with no indication at all of any problems. So I shut the thing off; jettisoned the remainder of my fuel; came down and picked up my two chasers, Bob Hoover and Dick Frost; and landed on the lake bed.

Jack Ridley and I wrote the flight test report on how we had gotten the airplane up to .84 Mach and sent the flight test report back to Wright Field. In the return mail came a very hot letter from Al Boyd wanting to know why I had exceeded .82 Mach when he specifically told me not to. Jack Ridley and I sat down practically all night trying to figure out how to answer the old man, because he was a pretty tough cookie when it came to discipline. I told him that the airplane had felt good, that I had exceeded .82 Mach because I felt nothing was going to happen, and that I was a little bit elated in flying the X-1 under power for the first time and so on and so on. He bought it, but in a terse telephone call told me to pay attention to what I was doing. So we went on.

For days at a time we followed the same procedure. The X-1 would be backed down into a concrete pit that had been built at the staging area. Then the B-29 would be towed over it and the X-1 was hoisted up into the bomb bay of the B-29 and hooked on to the bomb shackles. After getting it hooked on, the B-29 was backed off the pit and pulled between the two tanks that held the ethyl alcohol mixture and liquid oxygen with which the X-1 was fueled. The X-1 carried some 288 gallons of liquid oxygen and approximately 300 gallons of a mixture of five parts alcohol to one part water.

For the power source in the X-1, we did not have hydraulic pumps or generators run by auxiliary power units or hydrogen peroxide generators such as we had in later aircraft like the X-1A, X-2, X-15, and some of our space vehicles. The X-1's source of power was a very high-pressure nitrogen gas that was pumped into small bottles that were manifolded together. To get high pressure, some 5,000 psi, we used liquid nitrogen and boiled it through an evaporator to increase the pressure and pressurize the manifold. To use the 5,000 pounds of nitrogen gas, we ran it through a series of regulators, each of which controlled such things as the gear, the flaps, and all the other mechanical systems, as well as cockpit flight indicators and

The cockpit of the X-1 was entirely functional. Nothing other than flight controls and research instrumentation was in the pilot area. There was no ejection seat, either. For Chuck Yeager, there was no way out of the airplane other than by crashing it or landing it successfully.

cockpit pressure. We had a 100 percent nitrogen environment in the cockpit. The Occupational Safety and Health people would not go for that today. We flew with one oxygen mask and one oxygen system in the X-1. There was no redundancy and no backup system.

Robert Cardenas All of us were in our twenties, out in the desert, more or less on our own. We did not know how to design a flight path. Four engineers recently asked me if we had computers on the X-1 project. I replied no, we had slide rules. Then how, they wondered, did you plot an energy maneuverability curve for Yeager to follow? I told them we did not know what an energy maneuverability curve was, much less have a computer to plot one. Then how did you do it, they asked. Simple, I said. Dick Frost told us the structural design limits of the airplane. Jackie told Chuck to hold steady at Mach .82 or .84, and at the end of his run, just before shutting down, to pull a 3G turn. This put a load on the tail and approximated the effect of a higher speed. He did this in increments and, finally, at Mach .88 or so, as he made his 3G turn, he began to get a pitch, an oscillation. What was happening

ABOVE: The X-1 is being worked on in the loading pit as the B-29 is towed to the mating position.
RIGHT: The X-1 did not take off like conventional aircraft. It was dropped at altitude from a mother ship, in this case a specially modified B-29. This concrete pit in the staging area was for ease in positioning the X-1 underneath the B-29. After the B-29 was towed to a point directly over the X-1, the smaller aircraft was hoisted by straps to a midships position and secured to the bomber with bomb shackles.

was the shock wave traveling across the surface of the horizontal stabilizer and blanking out the elevator where it hinges on the stabilizer, causing a loss of control for the pilot.

As the B-29 mother ship pilot, I had to get the X-1 up in the air safely. Not to mention the fact that Chuck Yeager was very protective of that airplane. My problem was the way the X-1 fit in the B-29's bomb bay. If I raised the nose gear even eleven or twelve inches on takeoff, I would scrape the tail of the X-1 on the runway and that would create sparks. With liquid oxygen and other volatile fuels on board, sparks could turn the airplane into a bomb. Despite this, I didn't mind takeoffs because I was able to take off consistently on three points.

My biggest worry was if I ever had to land with the X-1 still hanging there. You know Murphy's Law: If it can happen, it will happen. And it did. One time on a test flight the 2,000-pound bomb shackles did not work. Chuck was in the X-1 getting ready to drop and it would not drop. So I said, "Chuck, you better come on back up. We're going to have to land with it." He decided to stay with it in case of inadvertent release; if it broke loose with no one to fly it we would lose the airplane.

BELOW AND OPPOSITE: The B-29 pilot, Air Force Major Robert Cardenas, had to be especially careful to clear the ground slowly on takeoff; too steep an ascent would scrape the tail of the X-1 on the ground, making an explosion likely. The X-1 pilot, Chuck Yeager, would not be in the X-1 on takeoff. He would drop down into the cockpit after the B-29 had reached optimal altitude. The discolored area on the plane's belly is frost from the liquid oxygen fuel tank.

So he stayed with the airplane until we got down to 5,000 feet or so, at which point he could not fly it anyway, and he came on back up to the B-29. That was the best landing I ever made in a B-29. I practically rolled the gear onto the runway and I did not scrape the X-1's tail.

Bob Hoover For the X-1 program, the plan was that Chuck was to increase flight speed by small increments. He would have gotten there a lot quicker had he been given permission to do so, but the program was being spotlighted to such an extent that everybody wanted to make certain that it was done as safely as possible. Bell had been flying the airplane for a long time by 1947, and the results had been limited, because nothing had proceeded very quickly. Chuck's progress would have been much faster if he had been able to make the decisions himself. But those decisions were being made by Albert Boyd at Wright Field.

James Young Yeager's eighth powered flight, on October 10, proved to be an eventful one indeed. After attaining an indicated top speed of 0.94 Mach at 40,000 feet, he pulled back on the control column—and virtually nothing happened! The control wheel felt as if the cables had snapped. He had lost elevator effectiveness and, with it, pitch control of the aircraft. Though the craft still seemed to be quite stable at this speed, he shut down his engine, jettisoned his remaining fuel, and

prepared to land. As he descended toward the lake bed, however, a solid layer of frost formed on his windshield, and despite repeated efforts, he was unable to clear it. He radioed Dick Frost, who was flying low chase, about the problem, and with Yeager flying on instruments, Frost talked him down to a safe landing on the dry lake bed. He had to have felt a certain amount of gratitude for the foresight of those who had decided to test the rocket plane over the vast, friendly expanse. Nevertheless, he had rolled out on the lake bed with a feeling of dread. Aerodynamicists had predicted that, at the speed of sound, the XS-1's nose would either pitch up or down, and without effective pitch control, he would be "in a helluva bind."

Chuck Yeager After seven powered flights, I had worked the airplane up to .94 Mach. On the eighth flight, at .94 (indicated), at some 40,000 feet, I rolled the airplane over and pulled back on the control column and nothing happened. I could

The X-1 is dropped by the mother ship B-29 on one of the test flights. Engineer and test pilot Jack Ridley, seated just aft of the B-29 pilot, usually was the one to pull the release lever. These drops had never been done before, but they proved to be highly effective and improved the flight safety of the program immensely.

flop the control column back and forth and the airplane would not respond in any way. I raked off the rocket engines and decelerated to a point where I had elevator control. I jettisoned the remainder of the fuel, glided down, and landed on the lake bed.

Following that, I was a little bit worried about the outcome of the whole program. I had accelerated into a region where I had run out of any ability to control the X-1. We got NACA and all of the engineers together and had a heart-to-heart talk about what was happening with the X-1's control. We did have in the instrumentation panel some manometer pickups, small one-eighth- or one-quarter-inch holes on the wing a foot or two out from the fuselage. They also drilled these holes in the horizontal stabilizer. They connected tubes from the holes to an internal recorder, recording the pressures in all of the holes. This pressure recorder showed that a shock wave had formed over the thickest part of the wing at about .88 Mach, as well as at the thickest part of the horizontal stabilizer. As we were increasing our Mach number, this shock wave would move backward. At .94 Mach, the shock wave was hitting right at the hinge point of the elevator. Under this condition, I had completely lost my elevator effectiveness.

I, of course, was most concerned because it was my neck that was on the line with the X-1. I talked to Colonel Boyd back at Wright Field. He told me that safety was the primary factor, so if I didn't like the program I could quit at any time. We would certainly call a halt to it if we had to, because the British had killed a pilot in

The X-1 shortly after launch, flying over the Mojave Desert near Muroc, in 1947.

After dropping from the B-29, pilot Chuck Yeager would ignite the rocket engines sequentially, and then would quickly outdistance the B-29 and the two chase planes.

their tests in the DH-108, the De Havilland *Swallow*. We did not want to jeopardize our whole research and development program by wiping out the X-1 and causing a lot of concern about our program here in the U.S.

James Young Postflight data reduction after the eighth flight, which included corrections for errors in the X-1's onboard instruments, initially indicated that Yeager had attained a true Mach number of 0.957. Subsequent analysis, however, later revealed a top speed of Mach 0.997 at 37,000 feet. He was getting tantalizingly close (and, indeed, there was reason to believe that he may have actually exceeded the speed of sound). Postflight analysis further revealed that as he approached that speed, a shock wave had formed right along the hinge point of the elevator on the X-1's horizontal tail. Fortunately, at NACA's prompting, Bell designers had provided the airplane with the moving tail that could, they hoped, serve as an auxiliary elevator. In theory, Jack Ridley believed that, dispensing with the elevator altogether, Yeager could probably control the craft by making small adjustments to the stabilizer's angle of incidence. This, however, had never been attempted at near-supersonic speeds.

OVERLEAF: **The lake bed awaits.**

A crowd of aeronautical engineers always observed the Muroc flights from the lake bed, waiting for test results to come back on the various individual systems they designed.

Yeager and Ridley ground tested the stabilizer system and decided that by moving the horizontal tail in increments of one-quarter to one-third degree, he would probably be able to maintain control without having to rely on the elevator. "It may not be much, and it may feel ragged to you up there," Ridley explained, "but it will keep you flying."

The number one X-1 sits on the lake bed after landing. The pilot's door has been removed. There was no ejection system on the X-1. This door was the only way in and out of the airplane. By this time, Chuck Yeager had christened the airplane *Glamorous Glennis*, after his wife, as he had done with his fighter aircraft in World War II.

Bob Hoover As everybody knows, Jackie Ridley and Chuck Yeager decided to use the movable tail on the X-1 so that the stabilizer could be manipulated, which gave him the controllability that was needed to break the sound barrier. Jackie was primarily responsible for that decision. He was just a down-to-earth, great fellow, very soft spoken, very calm, and along with it, a very good aviator—very precise and very knowledgeable. He gave us a lot of confidence. If Jackie told me something was okay, I knew it was.

Chuck Yeager We looked hard at all the systems on the X-1. It occurred to us that the capability had been built into the X-1 to move the horizontal stabilizer and change the angle of incidence. This, we felt, might solve the problem of the lockup on the elevators. We had not used this system during any previous flight. But we checked out the system on the ground and got it operating so that I could control or change the angle of incidence of the horizontal stabilizer in increments of about one quarter of a degree.

Chuck Yeager in the X-1. Although there were adequate sightlines out of the side cockpit windows, the view out the front was narrow. To make matters worse, condensation on the windshield from the pilot's breath fogged the glass, a condition that was alleviated by a thin film of shampoo.

Chapter Eight

The Day Mach One Is Broken

James Young Yeager had been edging ever closer to his objective and test team members were eager to put the "sound barrier" myth to rest, once and for all. The young test pilot was no less eager to get it over with. For this upcoming flight, however, NACA engineers had warned him not to exceed an indicated Mach number of 0.96 unless he was unequivocally certain he could do so safely. On the morning of Tuesday, October 14, ground crews completed their final preparations for the flight. They towed it over to the fueling area and backed the airplane down into its cross-shaped loading pit, moved the B-29 into position over it, hoisted the X-1 up into the bomb bay, and shackled it into place. A white layer of frost formed around the rocket plane's midsection as they injected the supercold liquid oxygen into the tank just aft of the cockpit. To prevent the recurrence of frost on the interior surface of the windscreen, crew chief Jack Russell had already applied a thin coating of shampoo to it—an ingeniously simple and inexpensive solution to a potentially dangerous problem. With the ground crew's preparations completed by midmorning, Yeager and the launch crew boarded the B-29 and within minutes took off from Muroc's main 8,000-foot runway.

Robert Cardenas Chuck was aware, as I was, that the four Ph.D.s on the ground thought we were going to kill Chuck and lose the airplane. I commented on this to Chuck. I said, "Chuck, if Ridley's right, you're going to be a hero. But if he's wrong, you're going to be dead. I don't mind making a decision but, on the other hand, it's your life." All Chuck said was, "If Jackie thinks I can do it, I'll do it. Somebody's got to do it, so I'll do it." I said, "Okay, fine."

James Young About midway through the B-29's long, slow ascent to launch altitude, Yeager made his way painfully down through the hatch on the right side of the X-1's cockpit. Over the weekend, he had suffered a pair of broken ribs in a

B-29 pilot Bob Cardenas had a tricky job taking off with the X-1 underneath. His angle of ascent off the runway had to be gradual, so that the tail of the X-1 did not make contact with the ground. Anything less than a three-point takeoff would invite sparks that could ignite the X-1 like a bomb. That is one reason why pilot Chuck Yeager rode in the B-29 on takeoff, and lowered into the X-1 cockpit while in flight. Here the B-29 ascends in preparation for the fateful drop.

When the B-29 mother ship reached 25,000 feet, pilot Yeager maneuvered his way down into the X-1 by a series of steps and handrails. It was a tight squeeze. Once Yeager was in the cockpit, fellow pilot Jackie Ridley would hand the removable cockpit door down to Yeager, who secured it from the inside.

riding accident at Pancho Barnes's. Fearing that he would be grounded by the flight surgeon, he had gone to a civilian doctor off base and had himself taped up. He had confided this only to Ridley, and now, with Ridley's assistance and the aid of a ten-inch length of broomstick that provided him with enough leverage to lock the door, he held his breath and secured the hatch.

Chuck Yeager October 12 was a Sunday night, and my wife, Glennis, and I had gone to Pancho Barnes's place to take a look around. We were out horseback riding, which we liked to do out there in the desert. After dinner we had ridden out through the pasture gate, and while we were out riding somebody came along and closed the gate. We were racing on the way back, and I was in the lead and wasn't seeing too well in the dark. I saw the closed gate at the last minute, and I laid my horse down, but he missed the gate and hit the fence post, flipped, and threw me a few feet. I landed on my right side. On Monday I was really hurting. I went in to the doctor in nearby Rosamond, and he confirmed that I had two broken ribs. On Monday afternoon I went out to the base and met with Jack Ridley and told him about my ribs. The next morning the X-1 was already hanging on the B-29 in preparation for the day's flight, and the nitrogen system had been pressurized by the time I got there. There was no time to explain my accident to anyone else, so I got in the B-29. Once we were airborne I found that I could go down the ladder well enough and I could get into the cockpit. I had to bend over real tight, and it hurt, but I could handle it. When Jack held the door down, I had to take my right arm and raise it in order to lock the rollers on the door. I couldn't do it. I just couldn't get enough strength in my right side. I told Jack my problem; he was looking down through the window and said we'd just look at the thing awhile.

The lever on the door of the X-1 had a little slideout where two rods came close to each other, about six inches apart. Jack searched around and got a ten-inch broom handle, sawed it off, and brought it to me. When I got that lever started, I could stick the broom handle between the two rods and get a ten-inch mechanical advantage with my left hand and close it. When I did this I knew I would be okay, because there was no problem flying the airplane sitting in a normal position. It hurt a little bit, but it was no big deal. That's the way you solved problems in the old days.

Robert Cardenas The night before, on October 13, 1947, the phone rang in my home, and an unidentified voice said, "I'm sorry to bother you, but I know Chuck Yeager has a flight tomorrow, and it is very important that you know that I just finished taping his ribs this afternoon." I felt like saying "Thanks a *bunch.*" I thought, well, do I put Bob Hoover in his place? Chuck, in all the time that I knew him, in everything he did, he had skill. He took calculated risks, but everything Chuck did always came out right. Whether it was driving cars or shooting deer, he figured it all out ahead of time and it came out right. So I stayed with Chuck. Of course, the next day I saw Jackie Ridley handing Chuck this little broomstick. I knew what it was for. I did not want to confront Chuck, saying, "Hey, Chuck, I know you're taped," and all that, because I would just be passing a load to him like the

OVERLEAF: **The concept of dropping the X-1 at altitude rather than having it take off conventionally from the ground was a key innovation for the program. This solved the engineering problem of having enough propellant to launch the aircraft from the ground and still have enough left to fly the plane at a safe altitude for a modest duration.**

INSET: **This photograph taken from a chase plane shows the X-1 dropping from the B-29 while Dick Frost flies low chase in a Lockheed FP-80 off Yeager's left wing.**

telephone caller had passed it to me. I did not think it would be fair to put Chuck on that kind of spot. But I knew he must be hurting, because he was going to use that broomstick to lock the door. I did not say anything. I figured that if something happened, there would be only one person to blame, and that would be me. So we went ahead. Jackie did not say a word and neither did I.

James Young As Bob Cardenas continued his climb in the B-29, Bob Hoover and Dick Frost joined up for chase in their FP-80s. Yeager pressurized the propellant tanks, checked the jettison system, completed his checklist, and then waited. One minute prior to launch time, Cardenas asked if he was ready. "Hell, yes," he replied, "let's get it over with."

With that, Cardenas pushed over into a shallow dive, and at 20,000 feet, Ridley pulled the release mechanism and the X-1 dropped free into the bright desert sky. The drop, at an indicated airspeed of 250 mph, was "slower than desired," and the X-1 started to stall. As soon as he was able to get the nose down and pick up speed, he fired all four of his rocket chambers in rapid sequence and left Frost and Cardenas far behind as he began his climb. Accelerating upward rapidly, he shut down two cylinders and, anticipating loss of elevator effectiveness, he tested the stabilizer control system as his Mach meter registered numbers of 0.83, 0.88, and 0.92. Moved in small increments of one quarter to one third degree, he reported that the stabilizer proved to be "very effective." He reached the 0.92 indicated Mach number as he leveled out at about 42,000 feet. With perhaps 50 percent of his propellants left, he ignited a third cylinder and, as he tersely explained in his pilot's report: "Acceleration was rapid and speed increased to .98 Mach [indicated]. The needle of the Mach meter fluctuated at this reading momentarily, then passed off the scale. Assuming that the off-scale reading remained linear, it is estimated that 1.05 Mach [indicated] was attained at this time."

He had felt no violent buffeting or any other indication that he had just passed through a dreaded "barrier." Surprised and, as he later recalled, somewhat disappointed that "it took a damned instrument meter to tell me what I'd done," he remained supersonic for approximately twenty seconds before shutting down his engine. He coasted up to 45,000 feet, performed a 1G stall, and then descended in a quiet glide toward Rogers Dry Lake, where he joined up with Hoover and Frost before touching down on the lake bed just fourteen minutes after launch from the B-20. Postflight analysis revealed that Yeager had attained a top speed of Mach 1.06, approximately 700 mph, at 43,000 feet that morning.

Chuck Yeager After dropping from the B-29, we took the aircraft out to .96 Mach and stayed there in relatively heavy buffeting while the Mach meter was fluctuating around .96. As I accelerated, the Mach meter jumped from .96 to over 1.0. They must not have had a lot of confidence in our program because the Mach meter only went to 1.0. One minute it was fixed at .96, then it fluctuated and jumped off the scale. On extrapolation, it worked out to about 1.05 Mach. At that speed the buffeting quit, I regained a bit of elevator effectiveness, and the airplane flew quite nicely. I shut off the rocket motor after about twenty seconds beyond Mach 1.0 and

A color version of Hoover's historic shot. The diamond shock wave is not as visible in this photograph as it is in the black-and-white photo.

came back through the speed of sound, got into the same buffeting, the same instability, and the loss of elevator effectiveness. I jettisoned the remainder of my fuel and liquid oxygen and landed.

The date was October 14, 1947. We were quite elated that we had accomplished what we had set out to do with the X-1. There were a lot of happy people that day, including Larry Bell and Col. Al Boyd and all of the generals at the Air Materiel Command.

Chase pilot Bob Hoover took this photo of the X-1 as it sped past him in excess of Mach 1.0 on October 14, 1947. The diamond-shaped contrail of supersonic flight was first seen in this picture, which wound up on President Truman's desk the next morning.

Bob Hoover I remember the morning of October 14 very well. I had a Ford coupe, and Chuck and I were sitting in the car out of the cold, waiting for the airplane to be fueled. Somebody gave Chuck the signal and we got out of the car. I went to my airplane and Chuck climbed aboard the B-29 as they moved it out from the loading pits. We knew that he was getting close to breaking the sound barrier at that time. It had been a very gradual buildup. He might even have done it before but we didn't know it, because he was sneaking up on it so cautiously. This was not due to his own desire to be cautious, but because of his orders. It was a wonderfully clear morning; I was up above 40,000 feet. It was easy for Chuck to spot me because I left a large contrail. This was helpful because when he separated from the mother ship he aimed for that contrail, which would put him in the right location for the return landing on the lake bed. I could see him coming from behind and as he passed me I started taking pictures. We got the first in-flight photo of the X-1 flying past Mach 1.0 with the diamond shock waves streaming out the back of the airplane. The picture turned out real well; it was flown overnight to Washington and was on President Truman's desk the next morning.

We were aware, and Chuck was aware, that he had actually gone faster than sound. I did not get a sonic boom when he went by me. I don't recall that there was very much radio chatter because when Chuck headed back, I started downhill with Dick Frost, and headed for the lake bed to keep up with him. Chuck set up his pattern and landed beautifully, as always.

Afterward, we straightlined it, beelined it, to Pancho's, and the fun started.

None of us were aware that there was any secrecy associated with it, so the cat was really out of the bag by the time we were told that it was hush-hush. I always thought it was a disappointment that it happened that way because it wasn't until many years later that Chuck got the recognition that he so well deserved and should have had early on, compared to when it did occur. It was a great event.

Mac McKendry We heard it at the ranch. We heard the boom when it went out, and we assumed that that was the sound barrier, because they'd been saying we would probably hear something when they went through the sound barrier. That evening they came over, about seven o'clock in the evening. There were about seven or eight of them with Chuck. Chuck got up on the bar, leaning against the wall in back of him, with one foot hanging over the side of the bar. Everybody was toasting him, including Pancho and me. We were all so glad it was successful.

Jack Russell When Chuck did break the sound barrier, we were all hoping that he would do it on that day. When Chuck radioed that the Mach meter had gone crazy, we knew what that meant. Some people claim they heard a sonic boom, but I didn't hear it. We were jumping around in the tower and that was a happy moment. Down on the ground we had a postflight meeting. Everyone was excited. There were a few parties, and though it is now kind of a blur, I know that we were walking around on cloud nine.

The X-1 team and Air Force officers surround Chuck Yeager after his supersonic flight, October 14, 1947.

Date: October 1947

Pilot: Capt. Charles E. Yeager

Time: 14 Minutes

9th Powered Flight

1. After normal pilot entry and the subsequent climb, the XS-1 was dropped from the B-29 at 20,000' and at 250 MPH IAS. This was slower than desired.

2. Immediately after drop, all four cylinders were turned on in rapid sequence, their operation stabilizing at the chamber and line pressures reported in the last flight. The ensuing climb was made at .85-.88 Mach₁, and, as usual, it was necessary to change the stabilizer setting to 2 degrees nose down from its pre-drop setting of 1 degree nose down. Two cylinders were turned off between 35,000' and 40,000', but speed had increased to .92 Mach₁ as the airplane was leveled off at 42,000'. Incidentally, during the slight push-over at this altitude, the lox line pressure dropped perhaps 40 psi and the resultant rich mixture caused the chamber pressures to decrease slightly. The effect was only momentary, occurring at .6 G's, and all pressures returned to normal at 1 G.

3. In anticipation of the decrease in elevator effectiveness at speeds above .93 Mach₁, longitudinal control by means of the stabilizer was tried during the climb at .83, .88, and .92 Mach₁. The stabilizer was moved in increments of 1/4 - 1/3 degree and proved to be very effective; also, no change in effectiveness was noticed at the different speeds.

4. At 42,000' in approximately level flight, a third cylinder was turned on. Acceleration was rapid and speed increased to .93 Mach₁. The needle of the machmeter fluctuated at this reading momentarily, then passed off the scale. Assuming that the off-scale reading remained linear, it is estimated that 1.05 Mach₁ was attained at this time. Approximately 30% of fuel and lox remained when this speed was reached and the motor was turned off.

5. While the usual light buffet and instability characteristics were encountered in the .88-90 Mach₁ range and elevator effectiveness was very greatly decreased at .94 Mach₁, stability about all three axes was good as speed increased and elevator effectiveness was regained above .97 Mach₁. As speed decreased after turning off the motor, the various phenomena occurred in reverse sequence at the usual speeds, and in addition a slight longitudinal porpoising was noticed from .98-96 Mach₁ which controllable by the elevators alone. Incidentally, the stabilizer setting was not changed from its 2 degrees nose down position after trial at .92 Mach.

6. After jettisoning the remaining fuel and lox a 1 G stall was performed at 45,000'. The flight was concluded by the subsequent glide and a normal landing on the lake bed.

CHARLES E. YEAGER
Capt., Air Corps

This pilot report tells, in the no-frills language of flight test, the story of the breaking of the sound barrier. In paragraph four, pilot Chuck Yeager estimates that Mach 1.05 was achieved.

Robert Cardenas On October 14, history was made. Chuck got to Mach .96 or so and all of a sudden the Mach meter jumped off the scale and he went through it, with the tail trimmed to do it. Jackie and I were up in the B-29. We knew from Chuck's communication that he had gone through, and we were really happy. I slapped Jackie on the back and said, "You were right, Jackie, they were wrong." I orbited over the base because Chuck would make his turn around Santa Barbara, and he needed a reference point for the return. Chuck has eyesight like an eagle, so he did not have any trouble spotting us. He landed on the lake bed and we landed on the base, taxiing up in front of Operations. One of those Ph.D.s that thought Chuck would kill himself threw one of his books in the trash can and took hold of Jackie Ridley and said, "Lets go rewrite the book, Jackie!" We were celebrating while poor Chuck was sitting out there on the lake bed by himself. We had to send a dusty old jeep out there to hook on to the X-1 and tow him in. That's how Chuck came back, standing on the wing of the X-1. He had just done something for the first time in the world, and we were all very happy.

About one week after the historic flight of October 14, 1947, the Mach One team was called to Air Materiel Command headquarters at Wright Field in Dayton, Ohio, to brief the Air Force brass on the details of the flight and to receive compliments for a job well done. The accomplishment was still a secret and would remain so for several months. But a celebration was in order, and it took place on October 20, 1947, at the Biltmore Hotel in Dayton. Gathered at the Kitty Hawk Room were (*left to right*) Maj. Bob Cardenas; Roy Sandstrom (chief of design engineering on the X-1); Capt. James T. Fitzgerald, Jr.; Lt. Bob Hoover; Dick Frost; Capt. Chuck Yeager; Larry Bell; and Capt. Jack Ridley.

Chapter Nine

The Milestone Realized

James Young Remarkably, this major milestone had been accomplished within a span of just over two months. In the days before pilots could pre-fly aircraft in simulators, and after only three glide and nine powered flights, Yeager had pierced a "barrier" that many experts had long predicted would be impenetrable. In hindsight, the speed with which this goal was accomplished seems all the more remarkable in light of the circumstances under which the program was conducted. By latter-day standards, the accelerated X-1 test program was a model of simplicity. The total test team at Muroc never numbered more than thirty people—fifteen Bell, twelve NACA, and six Air Force personnel. Less that fifteen years later, by contrast, the X-15 test program would require the efforts of more than three hundred highly trained personnel.

Management of the program at Muroc was also remarkably uncomplicated—in fact, almost informal by today's standards—and left in the hands of young men, all in their twenties or early thirties, who were given a wide degree of latitude by their Wright Field superiors. In consultation with Dick Frost, Bob Cardenas, and Walt Williams, Yeager and Ridley had the final say about when to proceed and how far to proceed on each flight. In the complex flight test environment of today, just the safety review process for a hazardous mission can involve scores of people and require up to six months and literally dozens of meetings to accomplish. Lacking a formal safety review process and the encumbrances of a large bureaucracy, the key members of the X-1 test team simply sat down and, based upon the evidence at hand from the previous flight, decided among themselves what the parameters for the next flight should be—and they did so with an alacrity that belied the magnitude of their decisions. At one point during the accelerated program, for example, Yeager completed three flights within the brief span of just six days. In the end, the speed with which the program was conducted was, to a large extent, the product of its simplified personnel and management structure. A small number of men had been given an important job to do and they had been guided by a philosophy based upon the conventional wisdom that the shortest distance between two points is a straight line.

Bell Aircraft head Larry Bell greets test pilot Chuck Yeager after he lands the X-1A, one of the second-generation X-planes that were slightly larger and more powerful than the original XS-1.

Monsignor Sheen's
Story of Savior,
'Jesus, Son of Mary'
Turn to Page 8

CHARACTER
QUALITY
AMERICA
FIRST!
ENTERPRISE
ACCURACY

Los Angeles Examiner

AN AMERICAN PAPER FOR THE AMERICAN PEOPLE
THE GREAT NEWSPAPER OF THE GREAT SOUTHWEST

Reg. U. S. Pat. Off.
Examiner Telephone Richmond 1212

Examiner Building, 1111 S. Broadway, Zone 54

OFFICIAL WEATHER

VOL. XLV—NO. 11

LOS ANGELES, MONDAY, DECEMBER 22, 1947   R   CCC

Two Sections—Part I—FIVE CENTS

U.S. PLANE FLIES 900 MPH, BREAKS BARRIER OF SOUND

HISTORIC FLIGHT—Unofficial sources have revealed that this rocket plane, the Bell XS-1 has flown faster than the speed of sound. The historic flight reportedly was made more than a month ago at Muroc Air Base. The record was said to have been duplicated twice since. The powerful craft, launched from belly of a B-29, was first announced as capable of withstanding speeds of 1700 miles an hour. Speed of sound generally is stated as 760 miles per hour. XS-1 is propelled by rocket power.
—U. S. Army Air Force photo.

CRADLED LIGHTNING — A giant B-29 carries the Bell XS-1 prior to launching the small craft for its sky-blistering tests.

It was stated that the XS-1 had been timed by radar and had flown at 40,000 to 70,000 feet. Other photos of record-breaking craft on Page 3.

Wife Confident but Watchful on Test Flights

"He h a s confidence i n himself and in his ship, and I feel his confidence."

Dark-haired, 23-year-old Glennis Yeager sums up in those words what she feels as she watches her husband, Captain Charles E. Yeager, fly faster than man ever flew before—faster than sound.

Every time that he has taken the XS-1—or any other record-seeking ship—up for a speed test she has been there watching, usually from the end of the runway. At first she was worried. Now, although she knows the danger to "Chuck," she is as sure as he is that he will land safely.

TWO SONS——

Yeager, now 24, and "Glenn" were married February 26, 1945, in West Virginia, his home. They have two small blond sons, Donald, 22 months old, and Michael, 6 months.

Donnie goes unerringly for pictures of airplanes and pictures of "daddy-airplane."

"I don't know which word he said first—airplane or daddy," laughed Glenn.

Michael has no words, so far,

Continued on Page 2, Cols. 2-3)

Muroc Rocket Ship Reaches 70,000 Ft.

Expected Problems Did Not Occur; 2 More Hops Bared

Man has flown faster than the speed of sound, it was revealed yesterday.

Captain Charles Yaeger, 24-year-old ex-fighter pilot, rammed his Bell XS-1 rocket plane through the dreaded transonic zone of speed at Muroc Air Base more than a month ago.

Exact speeds attained by the needle-nosed little skyrocket, which is dropped from the belly of a B-29, have not been revealed by the air force. Unofficial reports placed the speed in excess of 900 miles per hour.

Since Yaeger crashed through the turbulence that airplanes encounter at the speed of sound— 760 miles an hour at 59 degrees sea level—two other pilots have done the feat in the same plane.

They are Howard Lilly and Herbert Hoover, test pilots for the National Advisory Committee for Aeronautics, the Government's air research agency.

Record Altitude Also Reported

The XS-1 also is reported to have flown at altitudes of 40,000 to 70,000 feet, which would break the world's plane altitude record of 56,046 feet.

At such height, it could only be timed by radar tracking.

To break the sonic barrier, the XS-1 would have needed to fly only 662 miles an hour if it were at 35,000 feet, since the speed of sound varies with temperature and altitude.

The bright orange rocket ship came through the tests unscathed by the hammerings of "compressibility," and none of the pilots suffered from the experience, it was understood.

Designed for 1700 MPH

The XS-1 was designed to withstand a speed of 1700 miles an hour, but aviation experts considered it unlikely that its present power plant will make more than about 900.

Expected problems of stability, control and structural strength did not materialize in the transonic range, unofficial observers said.

Findings of the supersonic flights will be incorporated in other high-speed planes being de-

January 5, 1949. Pilot Chuck Yeager executes the number one X-1's first and only conventional ground takeoff. There had been considerable rivalry with the Navy and its research plane, the D-558, in the fall of 1948. The Navy contended that the D-558 was a "real" aircraft, since it took off and landed conventionally. Pilots Yeager and Ridley configured an unusual fuel load to prove that the X-1 could do it too. Ironically, after the Navy tested the D-558 with a turbojet and rocket engine combination, it opted for an air-launch system of its own.

Yeager's flight through the sound barrier that morning had borne out Captain Diehl's prophecy that it was "just a steep hill," and though few people could fully comprehend its implications at the time, the young pilot had just taken the first step in a chain of events that would ultimately vault man beyond the atmosphere and into space. But it had other implications, as well. The X-1 convincingly proved the feasibility of employing experimental aircraft to conduct basic research, and in doing so, it spawned a whole series of subsequent X-series designs.

In its successful conduct of the X-1 program, the U.S. Air Force (which came into existence as a separate service less than a month before Yeager's historic flight) had demonstrated that the military services could, indeed, play a meaningful role in experimental flight research. It would build on this experience and continue to expand its capabilities across a whole spectrum of research disciplines. And, more specifically, Yeager's success in the X-1 fulfilled Col. Albert Boyd's expectations and legitimized the role that military test pilots would play in a wide range of future experimental programs. Finally, although the two organizations had not always operated in total agreement, the partnership established between the Air Force and NACA during the X-1 program formed the basis for a number of future important and fruitful collaborative efforts.

The XS-1 program also helped establish the destiny of an out-of-the-way place on the Mojave Desert, where the new breed of exotic research aircraft would continue to carry men into the future. The skies above would become a one-of-a-kind laboratory; a laboratory where, after Yeager's epic flight, men would continue to fly into unexplored regions; where, for the first time, they would pilot their craft past Mach 2, 3, 4, 5, and 6, and up above 100, 200, and even 300,000 feet. Man's first supersonic flight transformed an obscure, almost primitive place called Muroc into one of the major landmarks of aerospace history. Renamed Edwards Air Force Base in 1949, and designated the U.S. Air Force Flight Test Center two years later, it would become synonymous in the public mind with man's boldest adventures in flight.

OPPOSITE: **The sound barrier test flights were highly classified. It took a bit more than two months before the story broke in a Los Angeles newspaper. It came to the newspaper from "unofficial sources." It was not until June 15, 1948, that the Air Force officially confirmed that the X-1 had exceeded the speed of sound.**

Months after the supersonic flight, Chuck Yeager was personally congratulated by President Harry Truman at a White House ceremony. Here Yeager shows the Distinguished Service medallion he received from Truman to his parents, Albert Hal Yeager and Susie Mae Yeager, who accompanied him to Washington.

Pilot Chuck Yeager in the number one X-1 airplane. Public interest in the supersonic flight took off in the summer of 1948 when the Air Force officially confirmed that it had happened. By the time publicity shots had been taken, the program had evolved into the next generation of X-planes.

Jack Russell So many people had lost their lives going faster than airplanes had been designed to go. But most were doing it in dives, not in level flight. Bob Stanley had said, at the beginning of the program, that the X-1 was a supersonic aircraft, that it had the power, and that was all you needed. He was right. Breaking the sound barrier opened up a whole new line of thinking in fighter aircraft and bombers. It meant that, with the proper power, engineering, and control systems, aircraft could accelerate far past what was considered until then the ultimate speed. This changed our thinking on aircraft design forever.

Robert Cardenas Breaking the sound barrier was something that occurred at a time and in a place that was meant to be. I was grateful just to be a part of it. We all wanted to tell the world about it. But there was no media hullabaloo like there would be today. And when word got back to Albert Boyd and Walt Williams of NACA about the flying tail, they clamped SECRET on it and we could not talk about it. The word went out to the American aviation industry about the flying tail and what it could do for an airplane, and it helped enormously in the design of many airplanes that were on the drawing board at that time.

Bob Hoover Up until the time Chuck made it through the speed of sound, a wall, a barrier, existed in the minds of all of us in aviation. We had seen what could happen to an airplane when it got into compressibility. We'd never flown an airplane that was designed for that kind of speed. With the airplanes we were flying prior to that point, you could see compressibility. We'd photographed it; you could see the shock waves build up and the turbulence occur, and the controllability of the airplane would be limited. Once an airplane was appropriately designed for that speed, it's been smooth sailing ever since. At the time, it was the biggest breakthrough ever in aviation.

Chuck Yeager I went on to make some forty flights in the X-1. I took it as far as 1.5 Mach at 1,000 mph. The airplane got up to 70,000 feet. Later, after completing all of the flights, the airplane was retired to the Smithsonian Institution in 1950 [now the National Air and Space Museum, in Washington, D.C.] where it still hangs today, just as it was during its last flight.

Discovering that we needed a controllable tail or horizontal stabilizer to operate within the region of the speed of sound was the most important thing that came out of the whole X-1 program, other than the obvious relief in knowing that you could fly beyond the speed of sound without killing yourself.

During the entire X-1 program duration, the data that we were getting from our flight test work was being digested by NACA and given to all of the major aircraft contractors, such as Boeing, North American, Lockheed, General Dynamics, and Republic, which incorporated the data into their new aircraft designs. In 1953, when I went with Tom Collins and then Maj. Gen. Al Boyd to Okinawa to fly the Russian MiG-15, it was quite obvious to me that the advantage our airplanes, such as the F-86E, had over the MiG-15 was a trimmable horizontal stabilizer.

As time went on after the X-1 program, we developed the X-1A, which on

Col. Chuck Yeager, USAF.

December 12, 1953, flew to 2.5 Mach at 78,000 feet. Other research aircraft followed, such as the X-2, the X-15, and of course, our space program. The jet aircraft evolved into F-100s, which could fly at supersonic speeds straight and level; then F-104s, which could operate beyond twice the speed of sound; then the aircraft that we have today, such as the F-15 and the F-16, aircraft that can fly at supersonic speeds and pull 6, 7, or 8Gs and never bleed off speed. That is tremendous performance capability. The weapons systems have improved also, to the point that one can do virtually anything with a fighter aircraft in the way of air-to-air gunnery with guns or missiles, and air-to-ground with smart bombs, guided missiles, and the like. The jet aircraft that we started with back in 1944, the Me-262s and P-80s, thanks to our groundbreaking work in the X-1, have evolved into the highly technical, high-performance jet aircraft we have today.

It is my opinion that in the not-too-distant future we will develop even newer jet engines. These jet engines will have the capability to propel passenger-carrying aircraft to speeds of Mach 3 or Mach 4. Today it is not economically feasible to operate a supersonic transport with current engines and their high cost of fuel. But when new engines are developed, it will be quite feasible to design and build passenger-carrying aircraft that will fly four times the speed of sound, and will do it on a paying basis. Until that time, I'm afraid we are stuck with the wide-body jet family that operates in the speed range of .8 Mach—a slow speed but, ironically, the speed that was considered deadly fast until we broke the sound barrier.

In the late 1980s, Chuck Yeager, then a brigadier general in the Air Force, revisited the 6062 X-1, the aircraft in which he broke the sound barrier. The aircraft resides today at the National Air and Space Museum.

The Men of Mach One

BY JEFFREY ETHELL

The story of the breaking of the sound barrier is a story not of machinery, but of men. Here, in the latter half of the twentieth century, we have become accustomed to technology, automation, and the awesome power of computers. But in 1947 the best tools for scientific breakthrough were human brainpower and courage. The team of men who convened in the high desert of California in 1946 and 1947 in order to shatter the mythical sonic wall had plenty of both.

In the preceding pages, many of the men who played principal roles in the assault on Mach One have chronicled in their own words the events leading up to, during, and after that great day of October 14, 1947. On the fiftieth anniversary of the milestone, it is significant and appropriate that these men have gathered to present the complete record of the X-1 program for all time. What you will not read in their narratives, however, is the most fascinating talk of all: the personal histories of the men themselves, who they were, where they came from, what they did, and what they went on to do. Each of them is a hero in his own right, and collectively they are a legendary group.

The people directly or indirectly involved in the X-1 program can be counted in the thousands and include the executives, engineers, technicians, workers, and pilots of the Bell Aircraft Corporation in the decade of the 1940s; the administrators, engineers, and pilots of the National Advisory Committee for Aeronautics (NACA); the officers and test pilots of the Army Materiel Command (AMC) and the Flight Test Division at Wright Field, Dayton, Ohio; the personnel cadre at Muroc Army Air Field; and countless other people with responsibilities on the lower tiers and fringes of the project. Each of them played a role, and each contributed in his or her own way. But the project really resided in just a small circle of devoted men, and an even smaller team of pilots and crew members who comprised the inner core, the real heart and soul of the project. It is this group that put its blood and sweat into the X-1 program, and risked life and limb to see it through.

Who were they, these Men of Mach One? In my view there were seven men who counted above all others: Albert Boyd, chief of the Flight Test Division for the U.S. Air Force; Dick Frost, test pilot and project engineer from Bell Aircraft; Jack

Col. Albert Boyd was not simply an Air Force administrator; he was a skilled test pilot. Here Boyd lands at Muroc in June 1947 after setting a world speed record of 623.8 mph, the first air speed record held by an American since 1923.

Russell, crew chief on the X-1; Jackie Ridley, Air Force captain, test pilot, and engineer *extraordinaire*; Bob Cardenas, Air Force major, pilot of the B-29 mother ship, and officer in charge of the Air Force's Muroc test unit; Bob Hoover, the Air Force lieutenant who was the X-1 backup pilot; and Charles E. "Chuck" Yeager, the Air Force captain and test pilot who flew the X-1 through the sound barrier.

As of this writing, nearly half of these men have left us. Albert Boyd died in September 1976, Dick Frost in December 1996, and Jack Russell in April 1997. Jackie Ridley died in an air crash in October 1957. However, Yeager, Hoover, and Cardenas will be celebrating the fiftieth anniversary of the breaking of the sound barrier at Edwards Air Force Base in October 1997.

In singling out these men, we do not disparage or discount the valuable work of others such as Larry Bell, the head of Bell Aircraft; or Walt Williams, the chief at NACA; or Jack Woolams, the first X-1 pilot; or Slick Goodlin, the second pilot. Each of these men were not merely participants, but insiders in the development of the X-1 and the achievement of supersonic flight. The seven men cited above, however, were absolutely indispensable; they were the ones essential to the program, who were on the flight line every day during the roughly sixty days it took to make history.

Although **Albert G. Boyd** did not live at Muroc during the test period and was not on site as much as the others, he nonetheless was the man credited with making the X-1 project a success. He was an astonishingly good pilot himself; however, his contribution was leadership rather than flying. As an Air Force colonel in 1946, Al Boyd was head of the Air Force's Flight Test Division, headquartered at Wright Field. After the job of flight testing the X-1 fell to the Air Force, it was Boyd who scrutinized the list of available Air Force talent and selected the members of the team that would make history.

Boyd was an Air Force man from way back. He was born in Rankin, Tennessee, in 1906. After his second year at Biltmore College he was appointed as an aviation cadet in 1927. He completed primary flying school at March Field, California, in October 1928, and went on to advanced flying school at Kelly Field, Texas, in February 1929. For the next four years he held the only full-time flying job he would ever enjoy in his thirty-year Air Force career, serving as a flight instructor first at Brooks Field and then at Kelly and Randolph Fields, all in San Antonio, Texas. In June 1935, he graduated from the Air Corps Technical School at Chanute Field, in Illinois, then stayed on to serve as an engineering and operations officer as well as secretary of the school until June 1939. It was during this four-year period that he received his first exposure to the world of flight testing. One of his duties as an engineering officer was to evaluate the performance of aircraft after they had undergone maintenance or significant modifications.

In June 1939, Boyd was sent to Hickam Field, Hawaii, where he was assigned first as assistant engineer and then as chief engineer of the Hawaiian Air Depot. During this assignment, he demonstrated the extraordinary command and leadership skills that were to serve him so well for the rest of his career. Following the Japanese attack on Pearl Harbor on December 7, 1941, he was commended for his "courageous and loyal conduct" that morning and, within two weeks, for bringing the depot "back to a higher state of efficiency than enjoyed prior to the attack."

Promoted to full colonel, he was next assigned to the Fairfield Air Depot at Patterson Field, Ohio, in February 1943. While working in a variety of engineering, maintenance, and logistics management capacities, he managed to maintain his proficiency in the cockpit and remain current in an extraordinarily wide range of frontline military aircraft. In December 1943, he was rated current in more than twenty-five different aircraft, ranging from heavy bombers to fighters. In July of 1944, he became deputy commander of the Eighth Air Force Service Command in Europe.

In 1945 Boyd became chief of the Flight Test Division at Wright Field. Aeronautics was in a period of dynamic change, and Boyd was fortunate enough to preside over the transformation of the role of military test pilots into research and development. Up until this time, that role had been severely limited. Military test pilots had been confined to service tests of aircraft destined for the operational inventory, while NACA and contractor test pilots did most of the research and development work on new models. Boyd wanted Air Force pilots to be involved in this work.

Most of the pilots then assigned to the Flight Test Division were combat veterans, many of them fighter aces. But many were not cut out for flight test work. They lacked the patience and objectivity that Boyd believed were necessary for effective test flying. Under his command, only those who met his very exacting standards were permitted to flight test. Every pilot who entered the division had to prove himself before he was permitted to enter the Test Pilot School and engage in actual flight test work. Boyd was also convinced that, given the complexity of modern combat aircraft, the military test pilot of the future would have to possess more than just good flying skills; he would also have to have the technical background to understand all of the systems he was testing and all of the phenomena he was encountering in order to be able to translate his experiences into the very precise language of the engineer and designer.

The choice of chief pilot for the X-1 program was an opportunity to test these theories about test piloting, and it is ironic that the man Boyd ultimately picked, Chuck Yeager, had no academic engineering background at all and was known as one of the most daring (but most competent) pilots in the Air Force. Boyd recalled, "The decision was made that we wanted the best possible pilot and we also wanted a bachelor. We went over the capabilities of our men and narrowed the list to twenty. Then we called back each of the twenty for a first-hand interview. Chuck had everything. He was the man we wanted. Then I found out he had a wife and child. It was a shock but I had to tell him, 'It's no go.' I'll never forget the look on his face. When he came right back and said, 'Please, sir, let me fly her,' that was it. He won, and his name has gone down in the history books." Yeager's success in breaching the so-called sound barrier in the rocket-powered Bell X-I in 1947 put military test pilots squarely into flight research, and under Boyd's leadership, Air Force test pilots came to be considered true professionals and among the very best in the business.

While the general public may remember Boyd for his role in the quest for Mach One, Air Force insiders know Al Boyd as an extraordinary pilot in his own right. In a time period from 1945 through 1957, the U.S. Air Force did not acquire a single

aircraft that had not first earned his personal stamp of approval. He was "the test pilot's test pilot" and it is believed that his flying record is unequalled by any other military pilot in the world. By the time of his retirement, Boyd had flown an amazing 723 different airplanes, in more than 23,000 total hours of flying time.

This giant of aviation passed away in St. Augustine, Florida, on September 18, 1976.

Richard H. "Dick" Frost was Bell Aircraft's civilian project engineer at Muroc not only for the X-1 but also for the second generation of X-planes—the X-1A, X-1B, and X-1D. He was probably the most versatile of the men of Mach One. Frost was an experimental test pilot for Bell Aircraft and Stanley Aviation, and flew hundreds of different aircraft, ranging from the Bell P-59 "Aircomet" to the B-29 bombers. Pilots still talk about an especially harrowing accident in which Frost manually bailed out of a stricken P-39A, surviving what is believed to be the fastest bailout ever survived by a human. Dick Frost performed an amazingly wide range of jobs for Bell in the X-1 program, including: project engineering; flying low chase on all the test flights; training Yeager, Hoover, and Ridley in the intricacies of the rocket-powered X-1; training support crews and ground personnel in the complex procedures for handling the highly volatile propellants used in the X-1; and improving the efficiency and performance of cockpit details, such as visibility, access, and escape procedures.

Chuck Yeager tells it this way: "Bell gave us Dick Frost to be our instructor. That was one of the greatest things that ever happened because Dick knew the airplane intimately. That's how we started the program. We didn't just come out to Muroc and start flying it [the X-1]; we came out to Muroc and sat down in a little ol' hot room and listened to Dick Frost and watched him draw pictures. He'd tell us, 'This is how it works and why it works.' "

Two years after the sonic breakthrough, Frost left Bell and joined Stanley Aviation, where he was a test pilot and specialized in the development of a wide range of safety equipment that was badly needed for jet aircraft whose speeds were outstripping the old designs. He oversaw the development of supersonic ejection seats for the F-104, F-106, F-4, and vertical takeoff and landing airplanes; escape capsules for bomber crews; upward and downward firing ejection seats; and automatic gas-operated safety belts.

It was inevitable that this passion for invention would lead to the creation of his own company, and Frost Engineering and Development Corporation was founded in 1960. Aircrew safety gear remained a primary concern for Frost, and the company's improvements in lap-belt/parachute-harness release design evolved into the belt systems now in use in many Air Force aircraft. Air mobility became important during the Vietnam era, and Frost Engineering worked on such things as cargo parachute release assemblies for the "heavies"—the C-17, C-130, and C-141 airlifters—and airdrop-extraction systems and components.

Dick Frost isn't as well known to the public, or to history, as Chuck Yeager or Bob Hoover, but within the aviation community he was a superstar. For the men of Mach One, far out in the desert in 1947, Dick Frost was the last word, the professor of flight. His intimate knowledge of the rocket plane and its systems was the umbrella that spanned the flyers, the engineers, and the crew, holding them all together in a common pursuit.

Dick Frost died in 1996, a scant year away from celebrating the fiftieth anniversary of the milestone he was instrumental in achieving.

Fame in aviation came to **Jackie Ridley** from both his legendary pilot skills and his brilliance as an engineer. Albert Boyd named Ridley to the Mach One team because he had all the essentials—he was a great pilot with great experience, and he had a knowledge of working aerodynamics and the ability to communicate flight concepts to everyone, high and low.

He was an Oklahoma boy, born on June 16, 1915. Following graduation from elementary and secondary schools, he entered the University of Oklahoma, and was later awarded a Bachelor of Science degree in Mechanical Engineering in 1939. In July 1941, Ridley entered active duty with the U.S. Army in the Field Artillery, where he served only four months before transferring into the Air Corps. He attended flying school at Kelly Air Force Base, Texas, receiving his wings in May 1942. His first assignment following graduation from flying school was in Fort Worth, Texas, as operations officer and assistant plant representative at the Consolidated-Vultee Aircraft Corporation, where massive manufacturing operations were under way to build America's fleet of B-24s for the war effort.

At the height of World War II in March 1944, Ridley was reassigned to the mecca of flight, Wright Field, Ohio, to attend the Air Corps School of Engineering, which was the forerunner of the Air Institute of Technology. After this advanced work, Ridley attended the California Institute of Technology at Pasadena from August 1944 to July 1945, studying aeronautical engineering with aviation pioneer Dr. Theodor von Kármán. There he received his Master of Science degree in aeronautical engineering.

After this extensive training, the Air Force wisely placed Ridley where he could put his skills to good use, at Wright Field, in the new Flight Test Division run by the formidable Col. Albert Boyd. Like Chuck Yeager and the other famous pilots of the era, he attended the Air Materiel Command's Experimental Test Pilot School, from January to May 1946.

After completing that training, the job of a lifetime naturally fell to him. The work of test flying Bell Aircraft's experimental rocket plane had been awarded to the Air Force, and Al Boyd was assembling a semisecret team to go to Muroc Army Air Field to break the sound barrier. Jackie Ridley would have to be a part of that team. He was just what Boyd wanted—a pilot with advanced engineering and technical knowledge, who could bridge the communications gap between pilots Chuck Yeager and Bob Hoover and the engineers at NACA. This was his very first assignment for Boyd—and it was a big one—to be the Air Force's project engineer at Muroc.

As Yeager and Hoover will effusively attest, the X-1 pilots did not make a move at Muroc until Jackie Ridley said it was okay. For every new test and every incremental increase in Mach goal, the pilots looked to Ridley, and if he said it was alright, they went ahead, and did so with confidence. Yeager has said of Ridley, "He had a marvelous knowledge of working aerodynamics and he was a real brain when it came to figuring out what the hell was going on with the airplane. Without Jack we would have been unable to accomplish what we did."

Ridley was even more important to the project on a conceptual level. There were many academics and NACA-based engineers who were very skeptical that the sound barrier could ever be broken. Data from their wind-tunnel testing seemed to indicate that drag at or about .90 Mach and higher would reach infinity. Ridley's numbers were quite different, and there were spirited debates between both camps even while the flight testing phase at Muroc was under way. As the X-1 edged closer to making a final run at Mach 1.0, the discussions took on some urgency. Jackie Ridley stood firm, as Bob Cardenas attests: "They [NACA engineers] arrived and Jackie got them in a room at the blackboard. I didn't understand everything he was writing on the board, but it was a draw. They couldn't convince Jackie and Jackie couldn't convince them. But since Jackie said it could be done, Chuck went ahead. He believed in Jackie and so did I."

Then, as is chronicled in detail in this book and elsewhere, Ridley's stroke of genius involving the use of the X-1's "flying tail" was another critically important decision, perhaps *the* critical decision that enabled the team to break the sound barrier. Yeager had flown faster and faster until he had reached a speed at which the normal flight controls of the airplane were useless. Yeager recalls, "We sat [idle] for three or four days, then Bob Cardenas and Bob Hoover and all of us sat down with Ridley and talked it over. It [using the flying tail] was Ridley's idea, because Bell had built in the capability for changing the angle of incidence, or angle

Jackie Ridley with flight test engineers.

of attack, of the horizontal stabilizer, which we had never used up to that point. Ridley says, 'Let's try and fly the airplane with the horizontal stabilizer rather than the elevators.' And we tried it out and lo and behold the tail was very effective." The rest is history, and the Mach One team knew that much of the credit went to Ridley. He was in the B-29 with Bob Cardenas as Yeager streaked past the sound barrier. Cardenas says, "When we were still airborne and we knew he had gone through the speed of sound, I reached over to Jackie and said, 'Jackie, you ol' son of a gun, you were right! They were wrong! Congratulations!' I felt I had to tell him that." The ramifications of this success were felt not just on the flightline at Muroc but throughout the aviation world. A whole new generation of airplanes came into being because of it.

If that wasn't enough, Ridley's legendary status in aviation lore was assured by a moment of pure picaresque, when he broke off the piece of broom handle that enabled Yeager to close the door of the X-1 after the pilot's now-famous rib injury. This ironic bit of low-tech repair may be the one Ridley story that survives all others, especially after it was chronicled so beautifully in the film *The Right Stuff*.

Jackie stayed on at Muroc for further testing of the X-1 and its descendants, and even got to fly the X-1. Yeager recounts Ridley's first flight: "We had had three or four engine fires up to this point and it was getting worrisome because you were sitting there ready for the thing to blow up, with all the liquid oxygen and fuel in the back. And ol' Ridley, when he dropped out of the B-29 and fired off three chambers and he's smoking out at about 1.01 Mach, there was a big silence. And he says, 'I got smoke in the cockpit.' And a few seconds later he says, 'The fire warning light's on.' I said, 'Jack, there ain't nothing in the cockpit that will burn,' meaning that it was pressurized with gaseous nitrogen, which is an inert gas. And he says, 'The hell there ain't! *I'm* up here!' "

Ridley rose to become chief of the Flight Test Engineering Laboratory at Muroc (later Edwards Air Force Base), and over time made huge contributions to aviation technology, including the basic testing techniques and philosophies of the Flight Test Center, which are now used in all test flight programs around the world.

In 1957 a planned reunion in Japan of the Yeagers, the Ridleys, Al Boyd, and Bob Cardenas was marred by the tragic death of Ridley, whose airplane was caught in a sudden, violent storm near Tokyo and crashed. The Flight Test Center at Edwards Air Force Base honors the memory of Jackie Ridley by having named its mission control building the Ridley Mission Control Center.

Jack Russell may have been associated with more aviation milestones in his career than all the other men of Mach One combined. As crew chief on dozens of experimental aircraft from the early 1940s until his retirement from the National Aeronautics and Space Administration (NASA) in 1977, Russell had a hand in such

Jack Russell and other ground crew members in back. In front, Yeager, Jim Fitzgerald, and Pete Everest.

milestones as the first U.S. jet flight, the first flight at Mach 2, the first flight at Mach 3, and the 199 flights of the legendary X-15, which still holds many speed and altitude records. The one milestone that clings most to Russell's record, however, is the breaking of the sound barrier.

A Buffalo, New York, native, Russell headed west in the late 1930s to become a mechanic for the booming Consolidated Aircraft Company in San Diego, California. A strike forced him back to Buffalo, but the prewar aviation building boom was in progress, and he caught on, first with Curtiss Aircraft, then with Bell Aircraft right there in Buffalo. Two years later, Russell was the chief mechanic on the famous XP-59 Airacomet, the first American jet aircraft. Testing was conducted at the secret complex at Muroc, California, where Russell got his first (but not last) taste of life in the barren desert. As World War II came to a close, Russell had finished his work on the XP-59 and had moved on to the XP-83, another jet prototype, and finally to the X-1 rocket plane, which was being built at Bell's New York facility.

In 1947, in an agreement with Bell, he was hired on by the Air Force as a civilian employee to continue his work as the crew chief on the X-1. Out he went to Muroc again. The X-1 was his airplane, and he had total responsibility for its maintenance and its proper working order. As in all aviation test flight programs, hundreds of variables and new problems cropped up every day, and a very inventive team was there to suggest solutions. But all of them were actualized by Russell, including the modifications to the now-famous flying tail.

Even the small problems, like windshield fogging in the cockpit, came to Russell. "We didn't have a very good system in there to get rid of fog on the windshield from the pilot's breath. We'd tried lots of things. Finally we tried some of the Drene shampoo, and it seemed to work. It put a film on the windshield that kept the fog from accumulating on there, and Chuck said it worked out fine for him." Yeager adds: "It wasn't but about six months later that Mine Safety Appliance came out with this 'new' discovery; it cost $18 a bottle and it smelled exactly like Drene shampoo."

The rocket engine was Russell's responsibility, too, and the pilots were always amazed at his ease around it. Without saying it in so many words, everyone thought the rocket motor was a bomb waiting to go off, but Russell worked on it with a mechanic's implacability. "I've seen him with his head in the inspection hole about two feet in front of the engine, with all four chambers running, trying to find leaks back there," says Chuck Yeager. "He'd put his head right back in there. We ran through a period of time when we had lots of fires in the back of that thing in flight. I'd come down and tell Jack I had a fire warning light and he'd say, 'Well, the nitrogen put the fire out. It's no sweat!'"

Russell's mechanic's soul shows when he talks about that engine. "With the power plant in that little baby, well, there was no doubt that we had the power to do what we wanted to do. Sometimes it would blow a cylinder off, but other than that, it was a sweet little engine to work on."

Russell gives much of the credit for Mach busting to the camaraderie of the whole group. "We had a great bunch of guys working on the program. Everybody was heading toward one point on this. We worked with NACA, with the Air Force, with Bell; it was a great team effort. They were all wonderful guys to be with."

But all good things must come to an end, and in 1950 Russell moved over to
the NACA side of Edwards to head their research in rocket power-plant systems. He
was part of the team on the D-558-2, which was the first aircraft to fly at Mach 2 in
1953; the X-2, the first aircraft to break Mach 3 in 1956; and the X-15, for which he
operated the launch controls inside the B-52 that dropped the aircraft.

After the last of the lifting body programs was successfully concluded, Russell retired to his home in Lancaster, California, where he now plays golf, travels the country in his RV, and has satisfactory memories of his participation in the most important
aviation milestones of the twentieth century. Jack Russell passed away on April 14,
1997, just six months to the day from the fiftieth anniversary of supersonic flight.

Robert L. Cardenas was Col. Al Boyd's administrative officer in charge during
the Muroc assault on the sound barrier. He spent the better part of his career, before and after the glory days at Muroc, flying for the United States Air Force. He has
many hours of combat flying time, and thousands more in flight testing such airplanes as the P-59, the YB-49, the Northrop Flying Wing, and the XB-45.

His risc to the rank of brigadier general started from humble beginnings, as a
private in the Army Coast Artillery. He learned to fly as a cadet in the Air Corps,
where he was commissioned a second lieutenant in July 1941, and six months later
found himself in World War II, eventually to fly B-24s over Europe. Like Chuck Yeager and Bob Hoover, he was eventually shot down in combat. He made his way
from Germany to Switzerland, then into France before the D-Day invasion.

Again like Yeager and Hoover, he became an experimental test pilot upon re-
turning to the States after the war. His specialty was bombers and multiengine air-

craft, and this was one of the reasons why he was asked to become officer in charge of the Air Materiel Command's flight test unit at Muroc. He would fly the B-29 mother ship that was used to ferry the X-1 to the height and speed it needed for air launch. (The decision had already been made to design the X-1 for air launch rather than ground launch. The extra propellants that would have been necessary to power the X-1 into the air from a standing ground start would have made the aircraft much too heavy. An air launch gave the X-1 the luxury of carrying only the amount of fuel needed for three or four minutes of flight. This lack of takeoff ability was always a bone of contention between the Air Force and the Navy, whose test pilots, especially Gene May, derided the X-1 as being only half an airplane. Eventually, after Mach One was broken, Jackie Ridley and Chuck Yeager had had enough ribbing, and they configured the X-1 for a ground launch, which they successfully completed on January 5, 1949.)

Flying the mother ship was no piece of cake. This was an entirely new way to get experimental aircraft into the air; there were few precedents. The difficulty was in taking off so gingerly and so flat that the tail of the X-1, which was slung underneath, would not scrape its tail on the runway. It required experience and a

YB-49 test team. Robert Cardenas is third from right. Cardenas would later pilot the YB-49 down Pennsylvania Avenue in Washington, D.C.

Cardenas by a P-80.

delicacy, and Cardenas had both. At least once Cardenas had to land the B-29 with the X-1 still underneath it, which required such a touch landing that the wheels of the B-29 could not depress more than six inches on landing or the X-1 would scrape its belly on the runway and possibly explode.

Cardenas was nominally in charge of the Air Force contingent at Muroc, but he had the good sense to know not to make the operation too military in attitude. As he put it, "I got very little guidance from upstairs. Everybody knew what they had to do. You never had to order anybody to do anything. They wouldn't do it anyway. You didn't have to. They just did it because they were there to do it. You got all the flying time you wanted. Very few rules and regulations. In fact, only one: No accidents. I thoroughly enjoyed those days because of the camaraderie that existed with everybody that was there."

Many people do not know that there was another Air Force detachment at Muroc at the same time as the X-1 team. The YB-49 Flying Wing team was there as well, and Bob Cardenas was named the chief test pilot in that effort in December 1947.

During the Korean War he was busy at Wright Field and Edwards AFB testing new jet fighters and bombers for combat use. When Vietnam became a U.S. war zone, he was already nearby as commander of the 18th Tactical Fighter Wing on Okinawa. During that conflict Cardenas flew F-105 Thunderchiefs, then returned to the States to command the 835th Air Division at McConnell AFB, training F-105 crews for combat in Vietnam.

More duties and more honors followed. He served as Chief of the Aircraft and Missile Programs Division in the Pentagon; was Chief of the Special Operations Division at U.S. Strike Command; was commander of the Air Force Special Operations Force; and was chief of a division of the Joint Strategic Targeting Staff, which was responsible for America's nuclear war plan. He retired in June 1973, but stayed busy with many projects, including President Reagan's Border Action Group in 1983, California Governor George Deukmejian's Juvenile Justice and Juvenile Delinquency Group in 1985, and the California Veterans Board.

OPPOSITE: **Maj. Bob Cardenas was a test pilot in his own right, but in his capacity as chief of flight test operations for the Air Materiel Command at Muroc he flew the B-29 that dropped the X-1. Cardenas retired as a brigadier general in the Air Force.**

Maj. Gen. Chidlaw and Bob Hoover upon his receiving the Distinguished Flying Cross.

Say the name **Bob Hoover** anywhere near an aviation nut and he'll tilt his head back, look up at the sky, and say, "Where!?" For many years Hoover has been *the* name on the air show circuit, including the big show at Oshkosh, Wisconsin, where a half million people reorganize their day if Hoover is going to be flying. He is considered the finest stick-and-rudder man in the world.

Like the others, Bob Hoover became interested in flying before World War II, then spent the war flying all kinds of airplanes. While he wanted desperately to fly in combat, he was denied that chance early on because he was, in effect, too good. Air Force brass kept him test flying all the fighter aircraft that were assembled overseas, to see if they had been built properly. Often they weren't, and only great pilots like Hoover could extricate themselves from all kinds of unusual mishaps. He finally saw combat in September 1943, flying English Spitfires, and flew fifty-eight missions before he was shot down and became a prisoner of war for a year.

By July of 1945, he was stationed at Wright Field, test flying in the Flight Test Division. He conducted dive tests on the P-47D in an effort to determine the feasibility of deflector tabs on the upper surface of the horizontal stabilizer to aid

Bob Hoover.

Bob Hoover was a test pilot for North American Aviation and has served as President of the Society of Experimental Test Pilots (SETP).

recoveries from high-Mach-number dives. Speeds in these tests were as high as .83 Mach, a speed barely attained in any previous Air Corps testing, nor even in the Bell phase of the XS-1 project a year later. Through this, Hoover had virtually unique knowledge of the aerodynamic force known as compressibility, and when the X-1 project came through, Hoover was on Al Boyd's short list of pilots. In fact, he would have been the primary X-1 pilot had Chuck Yeager not convinced Colonel Boyd to overlook his bachelors-only policy. But Yeager won the right to fly the X-1, and Hoover became the backup pilot.

It was not a source of friction between them; both had the utmost respect for the other's flying ability. Rather, it was a source of a lot of good-natured, fighter-pilot-style ribbing and competitiveness between them. Yeager recalls, "I had this old motorcycle and Bob and I were out at Pancho's one night, and I didn't have any headlights on this motorcycle and I wanted to drive it home. And Bob says, 'I'll follow you.' He gets in that Buick Roadmaster of his, and every time we'd come to a

Hoover and Yeager look at map of Edwards Air Force Base.

ninety-degree turn, he'd turn his lights out. Then he'd come and say, 'Are you hurt? Are you hurt?' He wanted to fly the airplane."

It was probably the only high-performance aircraft that Hoover never got to fly. Even after Yeager broke the sound barrier, the X-1 continued to be tested, and Hoover was scheduled to take a turn. But a freak accident in a P-84 and the severe leg injuries caused by his manual ejection (his legs hit the tail on bailout) put an end to his Air Force flight test career. Still, he is not the least bit envious of Yeager. "I wanted to be the first to make that flight," he says, "and I had hoped that I would have been. But it wasn't in the cards. I can only say, and I've said this many, many times over these last fifty years, there could never have been anyone who could have done it better than my dear friend Chuck Yeager."

Hoover has been known to have a lot of fun when he flies. His skills are so refined and effortless that it is easy for him to pull pranks in the sky. He even did it during the high-pressure days of the X-1 project. According to Bob Cardenas, "I always knew when Hoover was airborne because he had a little habit of coming underneath me and pulling up in front of my nose." Yeager concurs: "The X-1 was hooked under the B-29 with just a bomb shackle and that's *all* there was. I'd be in the cockpit concentrating on what I was doing, and ol' Hoover would come by about ten feet under the X-1, pull right up under the nose. And the whole B-29 would shake and the shackle would rattle. We'd exchange a few words." Hoover says, "I just wanted to let you know I was there."

For all that levity, Hoover was serious when it came to the X-1's rocket engines. He had seen the disastrous results of the Germans' experiments with rocket planes (for example, the Me-163 "Komet") during the war. "My biggest concern was the engines," he says. "Chuck and I saw the plane for the first time up at Bell, and it was a pretty awesome experience for the two of us. They showed us what liquid oxygen was like. They took a rubber ball and put it in the liquid oxygen and then dropped it on the floor. It shattered. They did the same thing with a frog and, I'll tell you, that got our attention. Then they made an engine run for us. The airplane was log-chained in a building, and when the rockets were fired, the ceiling started cracking and breaking loose and falling on us, and I'd never been so scared in my life. It was just absolutely deafening. I think Pard [Yeager] was thinking the same thing I was: What are we getting ourselves into?"

The respect continued once the airplane was being tested at Muroc. "It wasn't just the aerodynamics of going faster than sound. It was the handling of the rocket engines and keeping the dome pressures exactly where they had to be. Chuck was faced with not just flying the airplane but addressing all the dials and valves continuously. If he got those pressures out of kilter, he could have blown himself to kingdom come."

On the morning of the fateful day, Hoover and Yeager sat together in Hoover's car in the cold desert, waiting for the signal to go. Hoover would fly high chase, as usual, because he could get his airplane up higher than anyone. He got up to 48,000 feet, ten miles ahead of the B-29, when Yeager ignited his first rocket motor. "I had my head on a swivel watching for him . . . and he went by." Hoover's photograph of the X-1 as it flew past is now one of the most famous aviation photographs ever taken, because it not only documented the moment the sound barrier was broken, but also clearly showed the diamond shock waves at Mach 1.0 for the first time.

Hoover's aviation fame came not in one climactic moment like Yeager's, but was built over a lifetime of risky test flying (the XFJ-2 Fury, the T-28 trainer, and every type of Sabre Series aircraft) and crowd-pleasing airshow flying (three climb-to-altitude records at the Hanover Air Show). But the Mach One program is still a dear memory. "Being on that program meant an awful lot to me," he says. "I knew that it was going down in history."

In the same way the quarterback's name on a championship team will always be remembered more than anyone else's, the name **Chuck Yeager** will always be the one associated first and foremost with the breaking of the sound barrier. He was the man at the controls of the X-1 as it broke through the sonic wall. He is also the man who will tell you that the X-1 program was a team effort, and that the glory that has come his way is shared by everyone associated with the project. Here at the reminiscing stage, fifty years from the golden moment, you might expect Yeager to be sentimental about it. You would be wrong. Yeager has spent the last fifty years refusing to act like the big hero. He is matter-of-fact about his accomplishments. In his view there was a job to be done, the engineers and Jackie Ridley said it could be done, he was being paid by the Air Force to fly, somebody had to do it—so he did it. Even the exact moment of the sonic breach was taken in stride. The Mach meter, which was only calibrated to 1.0, simply went off the scale. Yeager said to Jackie Ridley by radio, "We have problems. This ol' Mach meter is plumb off the scale." No fireworks, no bands playing. Yeager, after landing the X-1 on Rogers Dry Lake, was towed back to Operations standing on the X-1's wing. He was happy, yes, but it was just another day at the office.

What else would you expect from a down-to-earth Depression-era kid from Hamlin, West Virginia? The Yeager story has been told before, in his own books and others, but the basics are these: After a boyhood of hunting, fishing, chores, and school, Chuck, like the other boys in Hamlin, enlisted in the Army. His instinct for machinery, learned at his gas-well-drilling father's knee, turned him into a fine mechanic. But flying school beckoned. He received his wings in March 1943 as a flight officer, a warrant rank. He joined the 363rd Fighter Squadron, and there met Bud Anderson, who has remained a friend and comrade-in-arms for over five decades. They went to England together in December 1943, and began a relentless series of combat missions in which they flew their P-51 Mustangs as escorts for the bombers flying to Germany and back. Yeager's luck ran out after only eight missions. On his ninth, he was shot down over occupied France. A French farmer put him in touch with the Resistance, which helped him escape to Spain. After a short while he was back in the cockpit, knocking down German planes. By the fall of 1944 the Allies' air assets had worn down a dwindling number of Luftwaffe airplanes, and Yeager and company began air-to-ground strafing attacks. Soon the war was over, and Chuck returned home to his wife, Glennis, whom he had married in Hamlin.

His next stop was Wright Field and the rigors of the Test Pilot School. His per-

Chuck Yeager in 1954, a true American hero and one of the world's greatest test pilots. Yeager is often quoted as saying that "duty is paramount for an Air Force test pilot."

formance caught the eye of Col. Albert Boyd, who added Yeager's name to the list of pilots he was considering for the X-1 program. After the interview portion of the selection process, Boyd knew he had his man. (A pilot named Gus Lundquist had been Boyd's first pick, but a depth-perception problem had cropped up for Lundquist, and Boyd took him off the program.) Yeager was selected as the Air Force's number one test pilot, and he, his backup Bob Hoover, and Jackie Ridley were sent first to the Bell plant in Buffalo, New York, then to Muroc Army Air Field to begin flight testing in July 1947. Bob Cardenas, selected to fly the B-29 mother ship, flew the B-29 from New York to Muroc on July 27, 1947, with the X-1 strapped to its belly.

Boyd had told the group he wanted them to approach Mach 1.0 in increments, but above all he wanted them to get the job done. The "job," in his view, was to break the sound barrier, and to do it with Air Force pilots, ensuring the Air Force's future participation in the flight test business. Yeager wholeheartedly agreed. He

was Air Force all the way. In fact, his service pride and sense of duty were his primary motivations for getting involved in the project in the first place. As he puts it, "This was the first time we military guys had been able to get our hands on a research vehicle. All research test flying was always done by civilian test pilots. And I was a very proud Air Force officer. Having fought in the war, duty meant a hell of a lot to me. That was the one chance we had, as an Air Force team, to accomplish something we had not been allowed to do before. That duty sort of entered into the whole thing for Bob Cardenas and all of us. That's the *one* thing that it meant to me. It said we hacked the program and it opened up a whole new era for us."

Yeager's career certainly did not end with the X-1. The qualities he displayed during the historic days at Muroc carried him onto a lifetime of aviation achievements. His flight testing schedule for many years afterward was legendary, often with twenty-five aircraft evaluations in the span of one month. By 1962 he had been named the Commandant of the USAF Aerospace Research Pilot School at Edwards Air Force Base. Over a five-year period he developed the curriculum and systems to train a whole new generation of test pilots, thirty-seven of which were selected for the U.S. space program; twenty-six earned astronaut wings.

He retired from active duty in 1975 but continued to flight test for many aerospace companies. The Air Force recognized him as an irreplaceable asset and asked him to serve in an advisory role for the Commander of the Flight Test Center at Edwards AFB. He has won every major award in aviation: the Collier Trophy, the Harmon International Trophy, the Fédération Aéronautique Internationale Gold Medal, and two of the highest honors his nation can bestow—the Presidential Medal of Freedom and a special peacetime Medal of Honor. An extraordinary lifetime of performance from an extraordinary man.

On the fiftieth anniversary of this milestone, it gives me and a nation of admirers great pleasure to honor this entire group of exceptional men. When will we ever again see so much accomplished with so few resources and so little regard for individual egos? The answer: We won't. Times like these don't exist anymore. The anniversary is a magnificent reminder of an America that once was, and a time that once was, and a place that once was, out on the high desert of California, where a dream came true fifty years ago.

Glossary

airfoil A structure, piece, or body, originally likened to a foil or leaf in being wide and thin, designed to obtain a reaction with the air.

airload Air pressure on the airframe caused by flying speed.

angle of incidence The angle, expressed in degrees, between the plane of the wing chord and the line of thrust.

Army Air Corps The Air Force was a corps of the U.S. Army before it became a separate branch of the Armed Services in 1947.

AMC Army Materiel Command, the command in charge of the Flight Test Division.

B-29 A World War II–era heavy bomber manufactured by Boeing; modified to carry the X-1.

bomb shackle A leather or metal strap used to hold racked bombs in place in the bomb bay of a bomber aircraft.

chord A straight line extending directly across an airfoil from the leading edge to the trailing edge; the length of the line.

compressibility The property of a substance, such as air, wherein its density increases with increase in pressure.

contrail The visible white plume behind an aircraft moving at altitude; a condensation trail.

critical Mach number The speed at which an aircraft's components or total assembly experiences a Mach 1.0 airflow condition.

drag The resistance to movement brought to bear on an airplane by the air through which it passes.

elevator A moveable airfoil, like a horizontal rudder, usually hinged to the tail section of an airplane, used to control horizontal altitude.

F Air Force designation for "fighter aircraft," as in the F-86 or F-104.

flare Rotation of an aircraft from approach glide path to landing altitude prior to touch-down.

fuselage The body of an airplane, exclusive of the wings and tail.

G/g The rate of change of velocity, when related to the "force of gravity." One G flight is straight and level unaccelerated flight. (To "pull Gs" is to make a hard fast change in aircraft motion resulting in a compression force on both pilot and airplane.)

glide flight Flight without engine power to test aerodynamics of the airframe without propulsion effects.

horizontal stabilizer In the tail section of an airplane, a horizontal airfoil that controls the pitch altitude in flight.

LOX Liquid oxygen.

Mach or Mach number The ratio of the speed of an aircraft to the speed of sound, at a given condition.

MiG Russian family of fighter aircraft.

nacelle An enclosure housing the engine of an airplane.

NACA National Advisory Committee for Aeronautics, the predecessor of NASA.

P Air Force designation for "pursuit," later changed to "F" for fighter.

pitch The degree or rate of flight inclination or slope, usually related to the horizon.

propellant Fuel for a rocket engine.

psi Pounds per square inch, a measurement of fluid pressure.

split S An aerobatic maneuver in which the aircraft is rolled inverted, after which a wings-level back-pressure on the control stick is used until reaching steady flight in the opposite direction.

stall The abrupt loss of lift on an airfoil.

subsonic Airspeeds less than the speed of sound.

supersonic Airspeeds in excess of the speed of sound.

telemetry Use of instrumentation on an aircraft. To measure selected parameters, transmit them to a radio ground station, and display them for engineers monitoring the flight.

thrust Forward force produced by escaping gases in jet or rocket propulsion systems.

transonic Airspeeds in the vicinity of Mach 1.0 in which instability may occur.

trim To balance an aircraft in flight by regulating the surface controls and tabs. To eliminate control stick pressure.

turbojet A jet engine in which the energy of the jet operates a turbine. To turn a compressor which pressurizes air into its combustor area.

wind tunnel A monitored chamber in which scale models of airplanes are tested to determine the effects of dynamic air pressure.

X A designation for an experimental aircraft.

XLR-11 The designation for the X-1's rocket engines, made by Reaction Motors.

XS-1 Experimental Sonic 1, later shortened to X-1.